This book has been designed to impart the knowle information needed to pass the UK Driving Theory safe driving practices and awareness of other road u

It contains knowledge relevant to safe driving and c relating to the Theory Test. Each chapter also has pic photographs relating to the subject.

It is advisable to cover one chapter at a time plus the relevant case study. There is one case study per chapter, however there are many reasonably priced Theory Test practice CD's on the market which would give additional case studies to practice on.

It is advisable after studying, to practice the questions and answers on the relevant chapter, then move on to the next chapter and so on. In the actual Theory Test there are 50 questions to pass the Theory part, the candidate would need 43 or more correct answers.

As similar questions are repeated through the official Theory Test in various different sections, so information throughout the book is repeated occasionally to re-enforce the knowledge and understanding required to gain a successful pass. Theory Test practice discs have generally in the region of 1000 questions relating to different aspects of driving, so questions can be asked in different ways. This book has been designed to give students the greater opportunity, to have more awareness of dangers on the road and to pass the Test successfully.

It is also advisable to be able to access a Hazard Perception DVD as candidates need to pass both the Theory section and Hazard section to pass the full UK Theory Test.

Learn to Pass the Theory – the EASY way! also makes reference to The Highway Code and Know Your Traffic Signs, these books contain more information and are recommended reading materials to support the learning.

The CPD Standards Office

CPD PROVIDER: 21085
2014 - 2015
www.cpdstandards.com

Accredited
cpd
Course

LEARN TO PASS THE THEORY – THE EASY WAY!

Ron and Carol Robertson

New Generation Publishing

TABLE OF CONTENTS

Chapter 1

BEING ALERT

1. Yellow lines are used on the approach to the end of roads to make you aware of the speed of your vehicle.

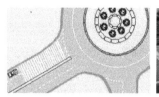

Yellow lines or bar markings used on the approach to ends of roads indicate that your vehicle should slow down, the markings can be used at the end of motorway roads, roads approaching roundabouts or junctions. They can also be used near hospitals, schools etc. They can be marked in different colours. Lines like these warn of an approaching hazard and encourage the reduction of speed.

2. Objects hanging from mirrors may distract attention from driving and restrict vision e.g. air fresheners, toys/mascots.

3. The following can distract your attention from the road;
   a. Loud music.
   b. Using a mobile phone.

c. Using a hands free phone.
d. Arguing.
e. Changing a cassette tape/CD/DVD.
f. Talking into a microphone.
g. Checking maps or adjusting/setting a Satellite Navigation System whilst driving.

Do not let passengers distract you as it can take your mind off your driving and can have dangerous consequences.

4. If you start feeling tired whilst driving, rest. Turn on the radio, get fresh air or a drink e.g. coffee, or walk if possible. It is advisable to drive for no longer than 2 hours then you should rest. If on a motorway, leave at the next exit or service area and find a safe place to stop and rest.

5. When stopping in an emergency, keep both hands on the wheel to control the vehicle and allow the vehicle to roll to a halt.

6. When doing a U turn in a road look around for a final check before moving off.

7. Always park before using a Satellite Navigation System, find a suitable place to stop before using the system.

8. If you feel that you do not have full observation when reversing, ask a pedestrian for help or get out of the vehicle to check.

9. When turning right across a dual carriageway, make sure the central reservation is wide enough for your vehicle.

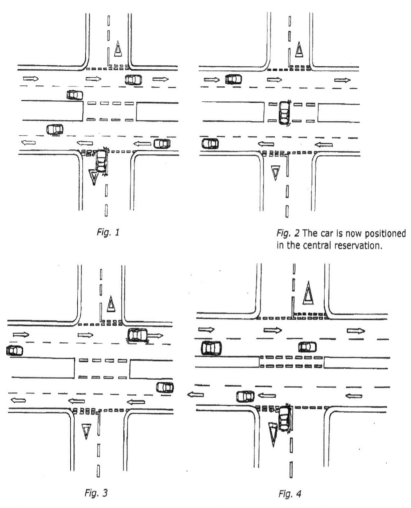

Fig. 1

Fig. 2 The car is now positioned in the central reservation.

Fig. 3

Fig. 4

Turning right across a dual carriageway (Figures 1, 2, 3, 4). When turning right across a dual carriageway as illustrated on figure 1, if the approach from the right is clear you may wait in the central area if there is enough room for your vehicle (Figure 2) until the approach from the left is clear. When safe to do so, proceed to complete the turn, Figure 3. Illustrated by Figure 4, as the central reservation is smaller, you must make sure both approaches from the right and left are clear of traffic and when clear you may drive across in one go, as there is not enough room to wait in the central reservation. Waiting in the central reservation would mean the vehicle would be blocking the right hand lane.

10. Be careful when emerging at junctions, there is often reduced visibility – blind junctions, car pillars etc., these can make it difficult to see other traffic such as motorcyclists and cyclists.

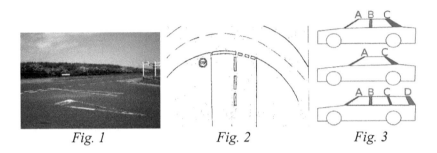

| Fig. 1 | Fig. 2 | Fig. 3 |

When emerging at junctions, make sure you can see in both directions before proceeding. If you cannot see, stop then edge forward slowly until it is safe to proceed. See Figures 1, 2, 3. Figure 3 is an illustration of car pillars that can block and hinder vision.

11. In some situations it may be wise to use the horn e.g.
    a. When coming up to blind areas.

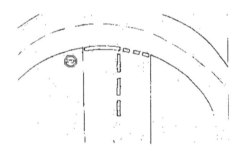

    b. At blind summits.

c. When people are reversing off driveways.

d. Approaching humpbacked bridges.

12. Places to avoid overtaking;
    a. Dips in the road.
    b. Bends.
    c. Bridges.

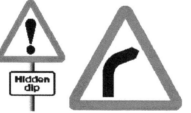 

13. When approaching a bridge in the road be prepared to use the horn as a warning - slow down, be aware of oncoming traffic or pedestrians. Also larger oncoming vehicles may be in the middle of the road as they may need to avoid the arch of the bridge.

14. Check your mirrors to assess traffic behind when you see a hazard ahead.

By checking the mirrors, you can decide what action needs to be taken e.g. you may need to brake and you may need to use hazard lights to warn other drivers behind of an approaching hazard. This could be for example on a motorway where you may be travelling at speed and need to reduce speed quickly. Assess how your actions will affect other drivers.

15. Before moving off - check all your mirrors, give a signal if necessary, look around and over your shoulder for a final check.

16. Before stopping, use your mirrors.

17. When approaching traffic lights that have been on green for some time – expect them to change.

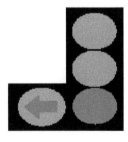

You are then ready and prepared for slowing down ready to stop.

18. Blind spot! this is an area not covered by the mirrors so be more aware.

19. If you get lost on a busy road, turn safely into a side road and check your map.

20. If you turn into a one-way street by mistake travelling in the wrong direction, turn into a side road and turn around to go in the correct flow of traffic.

21. When following a large vehicle e.g. bus/lorry, make sure the driver of the vehicle can see you in his mirrors. Do not drive too close.

22. Use dipped headlights when it turns dusk, even if street lights are not on.

Use dipped headlights when the evening starts to draw in, even if the street lights are not on. See and be seen.

23. On narrow country roads give cyclists and horse riders plenty of room.

24. Move back to left after overtaking. Also move back to the left when the arrows on the road tell you to.

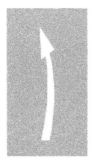 

The arrow tells you to move back to the left if you are overtaking because it may be warning you of a change in road situation. E.g. you may be approaching the end of a dual carriageway or you may be approaching a bend in the road, hidden dip etc.

25. Follow road signs and markings, they may also give you information about any hazards ahead and follow their advice - slow down if necessary.

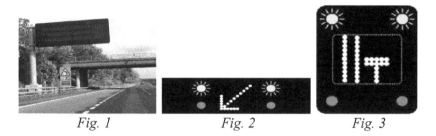

Fig. 1   Fig. 2   Fig. 3

Figure 1 the red triangle warns of an advisory speed limit of 30 mph on the bend, the overhead sign may have additional information. Figure 2 tells you to move to the lane on the left, possibly followed by Figure 3 informing that the right lane is closed. These signs are motorway signs but other similar signs can be found on A and B class roads.

26. Always be aware of vulnerable road users such as pedestrians, cyclists and motorcyclists.

CASE STUDY

Peter has a 3 hour journey to the city for a business meeting. He adjusts his Sat. Nav. before starting his drive. On the motorway he is careful not to drive to closely behind large lorries, and moves back into the left lane after overtaking vehicles. He continues his drive obeying the motorway signs but after driving for 2 hours starts to feel quite tired. He is ahead of schedule for his meeting so has plenty of time.

Q.1. Why does Peter adjust the Sat. Nav. before the drive?

Mark one answer.
a. He is not sure it is working properly.
b. Because it can distract from his driving if he adjusts it on route.
c. It is a new model and he is not used to it.
d. He has just charged it up.

Q.2. Why is Peter careful not to drive to closely behind large lorries?

Mark one answer.
a. In case they stop suddenly.
b. In case their load becomes loose and falls off the back.
c. He needs to make sure the driver of the lorry can see him in his mirror.
d. In case he misses his exit.

Q.3. What should Peter do to combat his tiredness?

Mark one answer.
a. Drive at a low speed.
b. Stop on the hard shoulder and rest.
c. Drive at speed to get to his destination faster.
d. Stop at a service area, rest and have a caffeinated drink.

Q.4. How would Peter know he was approaching the end of the motorway?

Mark one answer.
a. Warning lights would flash.
b. There would be speed humps.
c. Bar markings would be on the approach.
d. There would be a 30 mph sign.

Chapter 2

GOOD DRIVING ATTITUDES

1. Vehicle instrument panel may consist of the following;

Warning lights:-

Parking brake warning lights.

Braking systems lights.

Braking system - this warns of a fault in the system and requires attention. It could mean that the handbrake is on or that there is a fault in the system.

Main beam.

This light warns that the main beam is on.

Oil.

This is to indicate that oil levels are low and require attention.

Battery.

This will indicate a battery or electrical fault.

Indicators.

This light warns an indicator is still on. Your car may also have warning lights to indicate brake fluid levels are low. Petrol light - this may warn that the fuel is low. Other lights could warn that doors are not fully closed, the boot may be open or seatbelts are not fastened. There could also be warning lights for Power Steering - this will indicate that there is a fault with the power steering system or its' fluid levels and the ABS (Anti-lock Braking System) – will indicate that there is a fault with the ABS. In many new vehicles, warning lights are accompanied by a noise to also indicate a fault e.g. unfastened seatbelts, door not closed etc.

Other lights include;
Side lights.
Dipped headlights.
Fog lights (to be used when visibility is below 100 metres).
Hazard lights.

2.   Normal traffic light sequence.

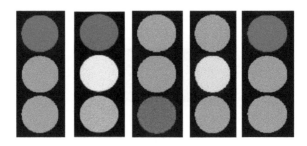

NORMAL TRAFFIC LIGHTS

Normal sequence is RED - then RED & AMBER showing at the same time - then GREEN - then AMBER - then RED. On a green traffic light, go if it is safe to do so, if the exit to the junction is blocked then do not proceed. On the amber, red or red/amber you must stop at the white line if safe to do so.

TRAFFIC LIGHT CONTROLLED CROSSINGS

The **PUFFIN** & **TOUCAN** traffic lights have the same system as normal traffic lights e.g. as above. The only different one is the **PELICAN** which has a sequence RED then FLASHING AMBER – then GREEN - then AMBER - then RED. A green filter arrow is for traffic filtering through in that direction. Do not enter this lane unless you want to go in the direction of the arrow. Give other traffic, especially cyclists more room and time to get into the correct lane. Cyclists should wheel their cycles across Pelican, Equestrian, Puffin or Zebra Crossings, they should never ride across. They are allowed to ride across Toucan crossings.

a. Pelican (has flashing amber).

A Pelican crossing stands for Pedestrian Electronically Light Controlled - it is controlled by the pedestrian by pushing the button on the box, this will activate the light system. The pedestrian will see a non-flashing RED man while the driver will see a GREEN light.

When the system is activated, the GREEN light the driver sees will change to AMBER then RED. At this point the RED man the pedestrian sees will change to a non-flashing GREEN man so the pedestrian can cross. After a time, the non-flashing GREEN man will change to a flashing GREEN man. This indicates that pedestrians are not allowed to start to cross the road, but pedestrians already crossing may continue. At the same time the driver's RED light will change to a flashing AMBER. The driver must wait if pedestrians are still crossing – if the crossing is clear the driver may continue. The lights will then change again – the pedestrian light back to a static RED man, the driver's light will change to GREEN.

b. Toucan (cyclists and pedestrians can cross at the same time).

The Toucan crossing stands for Two Can Cross, this refers to pedestrians and cyclists crossing together. On this crossing the pedestrian will see a man and a cycle, operating the same way as a Puffin, the pedestrian or cyclist will need to press a button. Cyclists may ride across Toucans whereas they should dismount at other crossings. There are NO flashing lights. Toucans are found on cycle routes.

c. Puffin.

The Puffin crossing stands for Pedestrian User Friendly Intelligent, it is intelligent because it senses pedestrians. The crossing time is varied depending on the needs of the pedestrian. So the GREEN man will stay on for the pedestrian to clear the crossing. The RED for the driver will stay on until the pedestrian has cleared the crossing - there are NO flashing lights, unlike the Pelican. To activate the system, the pedestrian will press a button.

d. Pegasus - equestrian crossing for horse riders.

These are found where a public highway crosses a road and in most cases there will also be a parallel pedestrian or Toucan crossing. The signals for a Pegasus crossing use a ridden horse symbol which shows as either RED or GREEN. They are operated the same way as a Toucan by pressing a button.

e. Zebra.

Note: Never wave pedestrians across crossings as other vehicles may be approaching.

This crossing will have continuous flashing AMBER beacons and is marked by BLACK and WHITE stripes on the road. Pedestrians should never cross the road within the zig-zag areas and drivers should not park on the zig-zag lines or go over the broken line. At queuing traffic, you must keep the zebra crossing clear – do not queue over the crossing. A zebra crossing with a central island is two separate crossings.

3. Drive keeping a safe gap between cars. Use the 2 second rule when on dry roads. Use the 4 second rule when in wet conditions and up to 10 times when in icy weather. Do not follow other cars too close (tailgating).

Rule 126: Use a fixed point to help measure a two-second gap

Drivers should always drive safely, if road conditions are dry then a two second time gap following another vehicle applies. If the conditions are wet, a four second time gap applies. Braking distances can increase by up to ten times in icy weather.

4. Lorries turning need space to manoeuvre, keep a safe distance as they may swing out across the road – known as lorry turning circle.

5. If you turn into a one-way street by mistake and find yourself travelling in the wrong direction, find a suitable place to turn around in a side road so you can join the correct direction of travel.

6. Flashing beacons on vehicles:

-Blue = Emergency.

    a. Police.
    b. Fire.

c. Bomb disposal.
d. Mountain rescue.
e. Blood transfusion.
f. Coastguard.
g. Ambulances.

Pull over safely and in good time to allow emergency vehicles with flashing lights to pass. (animal ambulances do not have blue beacons).

h. Green beacon for doctors.

Doctors displaying a green beacon may be on an emergency call so drivers should be aware and allow them to pass.

Yellow/Amber;

i. Breakdown vehicles e.g. RAC, AA, Green Flag etc.
j. Gritters.
k. Motorway maintenance.
l. Council vans, lorries etc.
m. Disabled scooters.

Flashing yellow amber beacons can be found on slower moving vehicles such as i,j,k,l,m.

7.   Speed sign for trams.

8.   When you fill up the car with fuel, make sure the filler cap is secure to avoid wastage, also spilled diesel can make the ground slippery. A loose filler cap can waste money and fuel.

9.   Different types of driving skills;

Considerate = good
Defensive = good
Responsible = good

Competitive = can be risky, dangerous and is bad driving.

Different styles of driving can denote how good a driver is. Good types of driving for example are considerate (considering other road users), defensive (planning and assessing situations carefully e.g. thinking and planning ahead), responsible (being responsible with the right driving attitude). Competitive (over confident, irresponsible, racing, speeding, inconsiderate etc.). Young, inexperienced drivers may show off and be competitive.

10. Be a patient driver - not everyone on the road obeys the rules. Try to stay calm and tolerant when driving.

11. When approaching unmarked junctions, slow down and check both ways as no-one has priority.

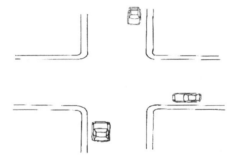

12. If bus lanes do not show operating times, then they are operational 24 hours a day. Do not drive in a bus lane as it can cause disruption and delays to public transport.

The above sign shows that the bus lane is not operational 24 hours but shows the times that it is in operation - between certain hours from Monday to Friday.

The above sign shows that bus lanes are operational 24 hours, but cycles and taxis are allowed to use the bus lane.

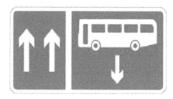

The above sign shows a contra-flow bus lane operational 24 hours the upward arrows indicate the number of lanes available to traffic travelling ahead.

13. If when driving on a country road you meet a person herding sheep, it is safer to switch off the engine and wait as animals can panic.

14. Be aware when passing horse riders or cyclists, horses can become frightened in traffic and riders can lose control - keep speed down and allow plenty of room.

15. When driving in busy traffic and the driver behind is driving too close to your vehicle, slow down gradually and increase the gap from the vehicle in front.

When a vehicle is following too close, by increasing the gap from the vehicle in front, this will allow more time for braking in an emergency, consequently allowing the driver behind to have more time to react.

16. Take up your position early when turning right to let people behind you know what you are doing.

17. Use the horn when necessary to make people aware of your presence. Horns are not to be used between 11.30p.m. and 7a.m. in a built up area or when stationary, unless another moving vehicle poses a danger.

18. When you flash your headlights, you make other drivers aware of your presence. It is a warning.

19. When driving in a one-way street, position the car in the right hand lane to turn right or in a left hand lane to turn left. Indicate your intention and take up position in good time.

20. Use dipped headlights when following vehicles on unlit roads.

21. Give way to pedestrians on a Pelican crossing when the amber light is flashing.

22. Slow moving vehicles should pull in safely and allow other vehicles to pass.

23. Cyclists and motorcyclists are at risk riding over tram rails because the rails are narrow and cycle tyres can get stuck. Wheels can also slide/skid in the wet.

24. At Puffin crossings, the red light that drivers see will stay on until pedestrians are clear of the crossing.

25. Slow down and give way to buses, they may pull out unexpectedly.

26. While waiting in a queue of traffic at night, use only the handbrake. Do not dazzle driver's behind with foot brake lights. However, when driving in fog it is safer to keep your foot on the foot brake which will give extra warning to the vehicles behind.

27. If a lorry is taking a long time to overtake, slow down to let it pass. Keep well back to get a better view of the road ahead.

CASE STUDY

Sharon is on a shopping trip in town. It is a dull and wet day so she has her windscreen wipers on and is using dipped headlights. She is careful not to drive too close to the car ahead. There is a pedestrian controlled crossing up ahead, the lights turn red so Sharon stops her car to allow the pedestrians to cross. It is a busy day and some pedestrians are still crossing when the light turns to flashing amber. Sharon waits until they have crossed then continues on her journey.

Q.1. What is the rule for having a safe gap between cars in wet conditions?

Mark one answer.
a. 4 seconds.
b. 2 seconds.
c. 6 seconds.
d. 10 seconds.

Q.2. Why has Sharon got her headlights dipped?

Mark one answer.
a. Because her main headlights are not working.
b. To make sure she can be seen by other traffic.
c. She switched them on by mistake.
d. She is breaking the law driving with them on in daytime.

Q.3. What type of traffic light system did Sharon stop at?

Mark one answer.
a. Pegasus.
b. Puffin.
c. Pelican.
d. Toucan.

Q.4. What light will Sharon see next after the flashing amber?

Mark one answer.
a. Red.
b. Green.
c. Red and amber.
d. Flashing green.

Chapter 3

VEHICLE SAFETY

1.   Environmentally friendly driving;

Plan your journey.
Use the internet.
Use route planners.
Use motoring organisations e.g. AA, RAC, Green Flag etc.
Use a map/atlas or a Sat. Nav. (Satellite Navigation System).
Choose the best times to travel to avoid congestion.
Avoid busy times.
Short journeys use more fuel (use a bike/walk/car share).
Plan an alternative route, your original route may be blocked.
All the above can make your journey easier and more environmentally friendly.

2.   Traffic can harm the environment as well as damage buildings through exhaust emissions. Heavy traffic can cause damage to the road structure and surrounding buildings. Traffic uses up natural resources e.g. oil etc., and creates air pollution through exhaust emissions. Eco-driving improves road safety and reduces exhaust emissions.

Eco-safe driving means smarter and more fuel-efficient driving. It is a new driving culture that makes the best use of advanced vehicle techniques. Eco-safe driving contributes to climate protection and pollution reductions.

The golden rules of Eco-safe driving are;

Anticipate the traffic flow.
Maintain a steady speed using the highest possible gear at a low RPM (revs per minute).
Change to a higher gear as soon as possible within the traffic situation and safety needs.
Check tyre pressures frequently.
Use air conditioning and electronic equipment in your vehicle wisely and switch off if not needed.

3.   Catalytic converters are found on the exhaust system.

A catalytic converter is a vehicle emissions control device which converts toxic byproducts to less toxic substances by way of catalyzed chemical reactions. Most present-day vehicles that run on petrol are fitted with a "3-way" converter, so named because it converts the 3 main pollutants in exhaust emissions into non-toxic substances. Catalytic converters are still most commonly used in exhaust systems in cars, but are also used in trucks, buses, motorcycles, airplanes and other engine-fitted devices.

They produce cleaner fumes. Road transport accounts for 20% of all emissions e.g. lorries, cars, heavy goods vehicles, buses, motorcycles.

4.   Driving smoothly can reduce fuel consumption by 15%.

5.   Driving at 70mph uses 30% more fuel than driving at 50mph.

6.   Missing out gears e.g. block changing, can help save fuel.

When accelerating more fuel is used, therefore rather than changing gears 1st to 2nd to 3rd to 4th, a little more acceleration e.g. in 1st gear, to build more speed then changing to 3rd gear means acceleration is used only once not twice.

7.   Using a roof rack increases fuel consumption.

Many vehicles have roof racks. Some are used regularly carrying bikes, luggage etc. The vast majority are empty. Aerodynamics can matter a lot at higher speeds (the more slippery your vehicle is through the air, the less your engine has to work to keep the vehicle moving). With the roof rack removed when not in use the vehicle is more aerodynamic and fuel efficient.

8. Late and harsh braking, short journeys, driving in low gears, rapid acceleration, under inflated tyres and poor planning can all increase fuel consumption.

Smoother driving and changing gears at the right time can reduce fuel consumption.

9. Planning ahead:- route planning, car sharing, vehicle maintenance, reducing speed, using public transport - all these also improve fuel consumption.

10. LRT (Light Rapid Transport) or Super Trams use electricity and are also Eco friendly because they do not use petrol or diesel.

This system reduces town traffic, reduces congestion and noise pollution, therefore they are environmentally friendly.

More people using public transport reduces the amount of traffic using the roads.

11. Dispose of used oil, batteries etc., responsibly. To be safe check your oil before a long journey. Take old and used oil or batteries to a local authority recycling site or to a garage for disposal.

12. Too much engine oil can cause leaks e.g. overspill.

13. Vehicle safety; park in a clearly lit area, park in a secure area. Hide valuables – lock away in the glove box or in the boot if you cannot remove them from your vehicle.

14. Older batteries may need topping up with distilled water to above cell plates if the battery fluid level drops - newer batteries may not require this as they are generally sealed.

Most batteries these days do not need to be topped up as they are sealed. Older batteries may need topping up when the battery fluid level drops. Check your vehicle handbook and make sure that the plates in the battery are covered with distilled water.

15. To keep your car safe, join a vehicle watch scheme.

16. Immobilisers deter theft.

Immobilisers are an anti-theft device using electronic security and will prevent the engine from running unless the correct key (or token/tab) is present. This prevents the vehicle from being 'hotwired'– bypassing the car's ignition to start the car without a key.

17. Do not leave documents or valuables in your car e.g. Vehicle Registration Document.

18. When you park your vehicle, engage your steering lock or use a wheel clamp.

19. Do not park: -
    a. Near a brow of a hill.

    b. Where a kerb is lowered for wheel chairs.
    c. At or near a bus stop.

d. On the approach to a level crossing.

Fig.1 shows countdown markers to a concealed level crossing. Each red bar represents 100 yards therefore, these markers show the distances are 300/200/100 yards to the level crossing.

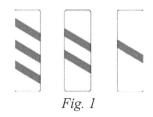

Fig. 1

Fig. 2 warns of a level crossing with no gate or barrier.

Fig. 2

e. In front of a property entrance. All of these may cause obstructions.
f. On zig zag lines.

20. When parking, use parking lights where the speed limit exceeds 30mph and park on the left.

When parking, use parking lights where speed limit exceeds 30mph and park in the direction of traffic. Your car needs to be visible to traffic on higher speed roads, so other road users will see the lights on the rear of your vehicle. In one way streets you may park on the right.

21. These warning lights on the instrument panel show faults in the braking system.

22. Unbalanced wheels can cause the steering to vibrate.

Unbalanced wheels will cause the steering to vibrate at certain speeds. They will require re-balancing at a garage or tyre fitting service to make the car safe.

23. A person is only allowed to drive **not** wearing a seat belt when they are medically exempt, or when reversing.

24. Road humps, chicanes, narrowing's, are all traffic calming measures.

Road humps, chicanes and narrowing's are known as Traffic Calming Measures. These are normally found in built up areas to improve the road safety. When approaching speed/road humps – slow down and drive over slowly. Road narrowing's are where parts of the pavements in streets have been extended and road markings or upright signs inform the drivers to wait and let oncoming traffic pass. This can occur in both directions to assist safety in built up areas. A reduced speed limit of 20mph is also often in force at the same time especially in narrow residential streets. Chicanes are road layouts used to alert drivers to slow down, they are present near schools, hospitals etc.

25. If there are problems with the shock absorbers in your vehicle, when you press down on a front corner of the car it will continue to bounce.

26. When carrying a baby in the front seat you must de-activate the airbag.

If the airbag is not de-activated and a crash occurs, the baby is in serious danger of harm from the inflating airbag. It is also illegal if it is not de-activated.

27. The car driver is responsible to make sure children under 14 years old wear a seat belt.

28. If you are transporting a 5-year-old in the back seat of a car who is under 1.35 metres /4 ft. 5ins in height and a child seat is not available, then the child must wear an adult seat belt.

The first picture shows a booster seat which can be used in a car with an adult seat belt if there are no child seats available.

29. Brake fade, the main cause is brakes overheating.

Brake fade occurs when the brakes are in continuous use and the brakes begin to overheat and braking power is lost. This is why when travelling down steep inclines for a longer period of time, a lower gear should be used to assist with engine braking.

30. Avoiding busy times when planning a journey can make it a more pleasant journey.

31. Never leave your car unattended with the engine running.

32. Under-inflated tyres can affect braking and steering. It can increase fuel consumption and make steering heavy.

33. A security-coded radio can help prevent theft.

34. Etch your car registration number/chassis number on the car windows to help prevent theft.

35. Red traffic routes help traffic flow.

*Red traffic routes are where yellow waiting restriction lines are **replaced** by red lines which means **no stopping for any purpose**, not even to pick up or set down passengers, unless by a licensed taxi. A driver displaying a Blue Badge in their vehicle may set down or pick up a disabled passenger **but** may not park. There are often Red Route signs accompanying the lines which will outline what you can or cannot do within the Red Route. Some Red Routes have upright signs without any road markings, these are designated as Red Route Clearways where stopping is not allowed AT ALL TIMES except in marked lay-bys.*

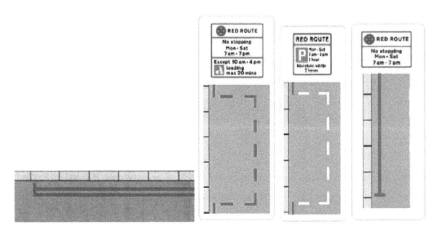

36. Do not sound your horn in a built-up area between 11.30p.m. and 7.00a.m.

37. Correctly adjusted head restraints help avoid neck injury.

38. It is illegal to drive with a deep cut in the side wall of a tyre.

39. Minimum tread depth for tyres is 1.6 mm, it is advisable to check regularly. This includes any vehicle e.g. trailer tyres etc.

40. Do not allow brake fluid to get low.

41. The law requires you to keep windscreen, headlights and seatbelts in good condition.

42. Faults in the braking system and suspension can cause excessive and uneven tyre wear.

43. Check tyre pressures when they are cold. Refer to the vehicle handbook for correct pressures.

44. Turning the steering wheel when the vehicle is stationary can damage steering and tyres e.g. dry steering.

45. If your anti-lock braking system warning light (ABS) comes on, get your brakes checked immediately.

46. In the M.O.T. emission tests are carried out to ensure your vehicle's engine is working efficiently. If not serviced regularly it may fail the M.O.T.

47. When driving wear suitable footwear to control the pedals and for safety.

48. Check oil level before starting on a long journey.

CASE STUDY

Brian is preparing to take his family on holiday. He checks the tyres, brake fluid, lights, oil and water, then checks to see if there are any problems with the shock absorbers on the car. He then de-activates the air bag before his wife straps the baby into a baby seat and secures it into the front car seat for the journey. She gets into the back of the car with their 12-year-old daughter.

Q.1. What is the minimum tread depth for tyres?
Mark one answer.

a. 1.4mm.
b. 1.5mm.
c. 1.6mm.
d. 1.3mm.

Q.2. If tyres are under-inflated what would it mainly affect?
Mark one answer.

a. Braking and steering.
b. Your speed.
c. Acceleration.
d. Engine coolant level.

Q.3. How can you check for problems with shock absorbers?
Mark one answer.

a. Rock the car backwards and forwards.
b. Press down on the front corner of the car, to see if it continues to bounce.
c. Open and shut the boot a few times.
d. Brake hard.

Q.4. Why does Brian de-activate the airbag?
Mark one answer.

a. To make more room in the front of the car.
b. To make the car easier to drive.
c. To protect the baby from harm if the car is involved in an accident.
d. To save fuel.

Chapter 4

UNDERSTANDING SAFETY MARGINS

1. Anti-lock brakes help prevent skidding in bad weather.

*Anti-lock brakes (ABS) activate automatically when maximum pressure is applied in an emergency. If you are driving a vehicle with ABS; apply the foot brake rapidly and firmly. Do not release the brake pedal until you have stopped. ABS does not reduce your stopping distance but you can continue to steer while braking because the wheels will not lock. The ABS will activate when the brakes are about to lock. ABS **does not** remove the need for good driving practices such as anticipation and correct speed for the conditions.*

2. The most common reason for skidding is Driver Error e.g. the driver misjudging a situation. Other common reasons for skidding;

    a. Weather (ice, snow, black ice, wet surfaces etc.)
    b. Road surfaces - uneven, loose chippings/stones.
    c. Hot surfaces in hot weather, hot weather can affect braking and the grip of the tyres.
    d. Worn tyres.
    e. Badly adjusted brakes.

3. Steering may feel light on ice and tyres make little or no sound e.g. on black ice.

4. If your car starts to skid on icy roads, try to correct the skid. If the back of the car skids to the left, steer into the left. If the back of the car skids to the right, then steer into the right. "Steer into the skid".

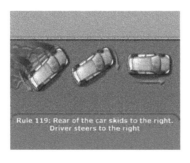

Rule 119: Rear of the car skids to the right. Driver steers to the right

5. Aquaplaning is when the car is skidding on water.

Aquaplaning can occur in or after heavy rain, water can prevent tyres from gripping the road surface. This may result in the steering feeling light with poor or no control. In effect the tyres are skating on water (beginning to aquaplane). To regain control, ease off the accelerator/gas pedal. Try to avoid braking as this may make the car skid!

6. In snow, drive at a slow speed in as high a gear as possible. When necessary, brake gently and in plenty of time.

7. When tyres do not grip on the road surface the steering will feel light, e.g. on black ice.

8. In bad weather always wipe snow and ice off windows, lights, mirrors and number plates.

In bad weather always wipe snow and ice off windows, mirrors, lights and number plates to keep safe. If your wipers stop working or are not effective, be prepared to stop your car and wipe off the snow by hand.

9. Ford

This is an area where water may collect in the road. Drive slowly through the water in a low gear and test your brakes afterwards to help dry them.

Fig. 1

FORD - is a name given to water collecting in a large dip in a road. It is usually marked by a sign and sometimes a gauge to show the water level. Drive through slowly and test your brakes afterwards to make sure they are dry. Pumping the brakes will help get rid of any excess water. Fig. 1 shows a depth gauge.

10. Do not coast, this means travelling with the gear stick in neutral or driving with the clutch down. It reduces your control of the vehicle.

Coasting or free-wheeling is when a vehicle is being driven with the clutch down or in neutral. This will result in less braking and steering control. For example, when driving down a steep incline such as on country roads, a lower gear should be used and with the clutch up the lower gear will assist with engine braking. Therefore, the brakes may not be in permanent use and this will help prevent them from overheating. If a driver is riding the clutch (driving with the clutch down) e.g. coasting, then the hill will encourage the vehicle to travel faster and a driver may over use the brakes. This can result in the brakes overheating and braking power is reduced. This is known as BRAKE FADE.

11. To park your vehicle downhill, turn wheels to the kerb, put the handbrake on and leave in reverse gear.

12. To park your vehicle uphill, turn wheels away from the kerb, put the handbrake on and leave in first gear.

13. Side winds are more dangerous on open stretches of road.

Side winds can blow you off course so drive safely; this can happen on exposed roads. In particular, be aware when travelling behind cyclists, motorcyclists, or high sided vehicles, as strong winds can affect these road users. Keep your distance.

Fig. 1

Fig. 1 shows a road sign warning of side winds.

14. When driving into a right bend, keep left for a better view of the road.

15. Bright sunlight can dazzle and other drivers may not be able to see your indicators.

16. Keep enough room between you and the vehicle in front so you can pull up safely if it slows down or stops suddenly. Your overall stopping distance is the distance your vehicle travels from the moment you realise you must brake, to the moment the vehicle stops.

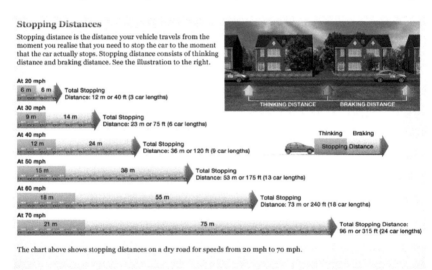

The chart above shows stopping distances on a dry road for speeds from 20 mph to 70 mph.

Stopping distances - this is made up of the thinking distance and braking distance. You need to be able to judge the distance. The figures shown in the picture for stopping distances are if you are travelling in a vehicle with good tyres and brakes and are driving in good road conditions and dry weather. A useful tip is to use a 2 second gap between your vehicle and the one in front, increase to a 4 second gap (double) in wet conditions and up to 10 times if driving in icy weather.

STOPPING DISTANCES IN FEET

SPEED MPH	THINKING DISTANCE	BRAKING DISTANCE	OVERALL S D SHORTEST S D MINIMUM S D
20 X 2	20	20	40
30 X 2.5	30	45	75
40 X 3	40	80	118
50 X 3.5	50	125	175
60 X 4	60	180	240
70 X 4.5	70	245	315

The above table shows the stopping distances in feet. The stopping/braking distance can be worked out by multiplying but this can only be done in feet not metres. The first column shows the speed the vehicle is travelling. The second column shows the thinking distance. The third column shows the braking distance. The fourth column shows the overall/shortest/minimum stopping distance. The thinking distance is always the same in feet as the speed being travelled. The stopping distances in column 4 can be worked out by multiplying by 2 at 20mph. Then increase by a half every 10mph increased. The above calculations work on all distances accurately except the shorter stopping distance at 40mph, this will be 118.

17. Sometimes temporary contra-flow systems are in place on roads/motorways. Reduce speed in good time. If the vehicle following is too close, increase the gap in front and if a driver cuts in front – drop back.

Contra-flow systems are used to divert traffic around roadworks and/or maintenance. Where a temporary contra-flow is in place you may be travelling close to oncoming traffic, sometimes in narrow lanes. This is why you must obey the signs and choose your lane in good time and keep the correct separation distance between cars. When traffic is at a very low speed merging in turn is recommended if it is safe to do so.

You must;

      a. Reduce your speed in plenty of time.
      b. Choose the appropriate lane in good time.
      c. Keep the correct separation distance when following other vehicles.

18. When overtaking a motorcyclist in strong winds, allow plenty of room.

19. Four-wheel drive vehicles have an improved grip which can help on uneven/slippery roads and improve road holding.

20. In freezing conditions avoid sudden steering movements – slow down.

21. In foggy conditions, allow time for your journey and use dipped headlights until vision improves. Reduce speed and increase the gap between you and the car in front.

22. Spray from large vehicles can reduce vision for vehicles travelling behind. Keep your distance and be aware.

23. Slow down approaching speed humps.

CASE STUDY

Fred is driving through the Lake District to visit his parents. It is a bright day but windy. He drives more carefully when approaching open areas of countryside and allows plenty of room overtaking a motorcyclist. He is also careful to indicate in plenty of time when driving through villages.

Q.1. Why does Fred drive carefully along open stretches of road?
Mark one answer.

a. To admire the view.
b. Side winds are more dangerous on open stretches of road.
c. He is trying to save on fuel.
d. To give him more time to use the mirrors.

Q.2. Why should Fred give the motorcyclist plenty of room when overtaking?
Mark one answer.

a. Strong winds can affect motorcyclists, cyclists or high sided vehicles.
b. To show off his car.
c. He thinks the motorcyclist is riding dangerously.
d. Motorcyclists always ignore the rules of the road.

Q.3. Why is Fred more careful about indicating in the bright sunlight?
Mark one answer.

a. He doesn't trust other motorist's actions.
b. Bright sunlight can dazzle and other drivers may not see his indicators.
c. He is not sure his indicators are working properly.
d. In case he forgets to signal.

Q.4. Why should Fred be careful not to coast and over use his brakes?
Mark one answer.

a. He wants to save on brake pads.
b. To avoid brake fade.
c. He may be low on brake fluid.
d. Coasting is eco-friendly.

Chapter 5

BEING AWARE OF HAZARDS

1. Do not drive under the influence of alcohol or illegal drugs. Also if you are under medication either check medicine labels, or ask your doctor or chemist if any medication you are taking affects you being able to drive.

Fig. 1

*AVOID alcohol when driving - **remember** alcohol affects people in different ways and makes some people over-confident, can slow reactions and creates poor judgement - all of which can cause accidents.*

2. Hazard lights.

Fig. 2

These may be used when the vehicle has broken down and is causing an obstruction. They may also be used briefly to warn following traffic of a hazard ahead. Fig. 2 shows the hazard lights control button.

3. Traffic calming measures are put in place to reduce the speed of vehicles.

4.   Amber warning lights (oval) are often found approaching school areas.

5.   Mirrors: flat interior mirror; flat mirrors give a clearer, truer vision.

Convex exterior - give a wider field of vision e.g. wing mirror.

Extended side wing mirrors are used when towing caravans and on long vehicles for better vision especially when towing.

6.   The following may make car insurance more expensive:-

a. Dangerous driving.
b. Driving under the influence of drink or drugs.
c. Driving without due care and attention.
d. Other driving offences if convicted.

Remember alcohol increases confidence, slows reactions, creates poor judgment!

AVOID alcohol when driving.

7. School bus sign, usually displayed on the rear of a school bus.

8. Projection markers on lorries etc.

Markers must be fitted to vehicles over 13 metres long when the load or equipment overhangs the front or rear by more than 2 metres. Vertical yellow/orange markings must be fitted to large vehicles but also to builder's skips left in a road. They are also reflective so can be seen at night to alert drivers of the hazard.

9. Give way to buses, they may not always indicate.

10. Sharp deviation sign – shows deviation to the left, right if reversed.

Sharp deviation signs are found before sharp bends and on roundabouts.

11. Spray from large vehicles can reduce vision for vehicles travelling behind. Keep your distance and be aware.

12. Use reflections in shop windows to see other traffic. This can help when your view is restricted i.e. when emerging from junctions and vision is reduced possibly due to parked vehicles or overhanging foliage.

13. Two way roads with 3 lanes. Traffic in both directions can use the middle lane to overtake. Do not overtake when approaching a junction or when your view ahead is blocked.

Two way roads with 3 lanes. On a two-way road where there are 3 lanes, traffic travelling in both directions may use the middle lane for overtaking. This may be restricted due to white lines painted on the road. Do not cross a solid white line on your side unless overtaking a vehicle travelling at 10

mph or less if it is safe to do so. However, you may cross a broken line to
overtake if it is also safe to do so.

14. Reflective studs sometimes known as 'cat's eyes' are used on
    motorways to mark different lanes.

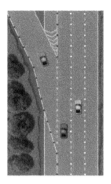

Fig. 1

Reflective studs are used on motorways to help drivers at night or in poor
visibility, they are often known as 'cat's eyes'. White studs mark traffic
lanes (Fig. 1), the left hand side of the carriageway is marked with red
studs (Fig. 1) and amber studs are found between the central reservation
and the carriageway on a motorway.

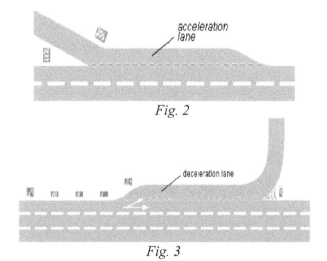

Fig. 2

Fig. 3

Green studs are used to mark lay-bys and the entrances to and exits from
slip roads (Figs 2, 3). Yellow/green reflective studs are used for temporary
adjustments to lane layouts for motorway maintenance. The acceleration

lane is the lane/joining slip road. This is where the traffic builds speed to join the motorway or dual-carriageway (Fig. 2). The deceleration lane is the lane/slip road leaving the motorway or dual-carriage way. This is where the traffic reduces speed leaving the motorway or dual-carriageway (Fig. 3).

15. Crawler lanes.

Crawler lanes are found on steep gradients. These lanes are for slower traffic and heavy vehicles. These can help prevent disruption to the normal traffic flow.

16. Normally overtaking on the **left** is not allowed. Exceptions to this rule are;

a. Allowed to overtake on the left in slow moving queues of traffic.
b. When the vehicle in front is turning right.
c. When travelling in one-way systems.

17. Motorway emergency telephones are normally linked to a police control centre but lately they have also been linked to the Highways Agency. *(Fig. 1.)*

Fig. 1

18. If you have a flat tyre and breakdown on a motorway do not attempt to change the wheel yourself. There are emergency telephone boxes to ring for assistance. Fig. 1.

19. ATM (Active Traffic Management controlled area)

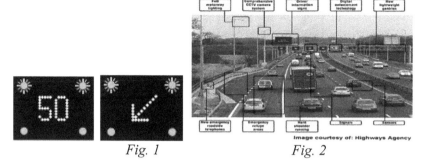

Fig. 1   Fig. 2

Fig. 1 & 2 arrows indicate that drivers move to lanes on the left.

Figs. 1-5
Active Traffic Management (ATM) Figures 1-5.

ATM consists of traffic monitoring, CCTV camera's watch for accidents happening on motorways.
Active traffic management deals with;
Accident control
Different/variable message signs
Controlling lane signals
Variable/different speed limit signs
Information for drivers
History of what has happened ahead e.g. incidents/accidents.
Figure 5 shows an emergency refuge area on the left.
ATM's are not present in Northern Ireland.

Contra-flow system.

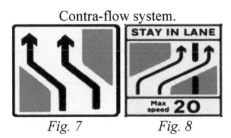

Fig. 7   Fig. 8

Figures 7, 8 show a contra-flow system on a motorway.

Contra-flow systems are used to divert traffic around road works or maintenance. Where a temporary contra-flow is in place you will be travelling close to oncoming traffic, sometimes in narrow lanes. This is why you must reduce your speed and choose your lane in good time and keep the correct separation distance from the car in front.

20. Keep junctions clear for access.

Do not block junctions - they must be clear to allow access to other vehicles and to allow traffic to emerge.

21. A disabled scooter may have a flashing amber light to warn other drivers. They are also restricted from driving above 8 mph. Mobility scooters travel more slowly than other traffic and may be less visible. They must use lights to be seen at night.

22. Keep a 4 second time gap in wet weather from the vehicle in front.

23. Ignore other driver's road rage or mistakes. Stay calm.

24. Staggered junction.

This road sign shows side roads off the main road but the junctions are staggered. It may be wise to reduce speed approaching this hazard as there may be vehicles emerging.

25. Inform the licensing authority (D.V.L.A. or D.V.A. in Northern Ireland) if your health deteriorates e.g. poor eyesight, epilepsy etc.

26. Tinted glasses or sunglasses should be removed before driving through a tunnel.

Tinted glasses e.g. sun glasses must not be worn when driving through tunnels or at night. When worn in bright sunlight then entering a tunnel your vision will not adjust quick enough and you will be unable to see properly.

27. Kick down.

Kick down is used in automatic vehicles to accelerate quickly. When driving an automatic car and quick acceleration is needed, the accelerator pedal should be pushed to the floor firmly, the gearbox then changes down to a lower gear to provide power for quick acceleration.

28. Learner car drivers (provisional licence holders) **are not** allowed on motorways and must be supervised when driving.

29. In different situations e.g. road traffic accident, signals failing etc., the traffic control police may be present, directing traffic using hand signals.

Fig. 1   Fig. 2

Figure 1 shows an officer stopping approaching traffic and traffic from behind. Figure 2 shows the officer stopping approaching traffic.

30. If you take a wrong turn into a one-way street, find a safe place to turn your vehicle around so you are facing the right direction, possibly using a side street.

31. On level crossings, the steady amber lights will show (not flashing) this is the first warning, then the lights may change to flashing red (Fig. 1).

Fig. 1   Fig. 2

In Figure 2 the red triangle sign shows a picture of a gate. This warns of the approach to a level crossing with a gate or barrier.

32. Elderly drivers may not have quick reactions – be patient and give them time.

33. When driving towards a left hand bend be aware that pedestrians may be walking towards you on the road if there is no pathway or pavement.

| Fig. 1 | Fig. 2 | Fig. 3 | Fig. 4 |

Figure 3 shows a sign warning of pedestrians on the road, this is because there is no pavement or pathway. Figure 4 is an edge of carriageway line.

34. Be careful when following a cyclist along a street, they could swerve out or wobble.

35. If you feel drowsy when driving down a motorway;

   a. Open a window for fresh air.
   b. Turn on the radio.
   c. Find a safe place to stop i.e. service station.
   d. Exit the motorway to find a place to stop and rest.

36. Do not read maps, use a mobile phone or have loud music on when driving. If you need to use a map or mobile, find a safe place to stop. Loud music can distract some drivers – stay safe.

37. If you are prescribed glasses for driving, make sure you use them all the time when driving.

38. Do not overtake just before turning left.

Here the picture shows a cyclist, in this situation you should stay behind the cyclist then turn.

39. Horns can be used as a warning to alert other traffic of a hazard.

40. When approaching a bridge, be prepared for lorries, buses etc. They can move into the middle of the road to clear the bridge. Road markings may indicate awareness of high sided vehicles. Other drivers should still keep to the left.

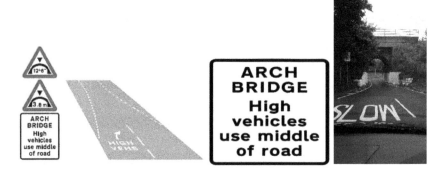

41. Slow moving vehicles may display a sign advising drivers to approach with care and keep to either the left or the right.

42. Place names are sometimes painted on road surfaces to prompt drivers to change lanes early.

43. Be careful when driving down a street with lots of parked cars, the hazards can be;

   a. Cars moving off.
   b. Pedestrians and children coming out between parked cars.
   c. Car doors opening.

44. Motorcyclists may wear bright clothing to allow them to be seen and may also give hand signals to indicate their intentions.

45. When driving be aware of road work signs, they are there to warn drivers to slow down. Obey the instructions on the signs.

Fig. 1   Fig. 2   Fig. 3

Fig. 3 indicates that the right hand lane is closed so traffic may move to the left from the right hand lane.

46. When driving be aware of junctions with poor visibility.

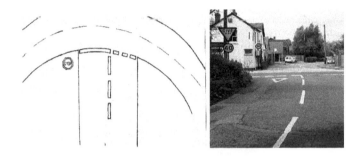

Be careful when emerging at junctions, there is often reduced visibility. Do not pull out of a junction unless you are sure of approaching traffic's intentions e.g. if an approaching vehicle from the right is signalling left make sure they are turning in. Blind junctions also car pillars etc. can make it difficult to see motorcyclists, cyclists etc.

47. Be aware of potential hazards at all times when driving. Hazard lines are placed to warn drivers and make them aware.

48. Advanced warning lines allow cyclists to position themselves in front of other traffic.

Advanced warning lines can be found at traffic lights. These are to protect cyclists. Vehicles cannot enter the area marked with the cycle, traffic must wait behind the advanced warning line. When lights change to green allow the cyclists to move away first. This red area allows cyclists to position in front of traffic.

49. A hearing dog for the deaf may wear a burgundy coat signifying that the person they are with is deaf.

50. A red x on a motorway means - do not continue in that lane. You must obey flashing red lights, these also tell you not to continue. If other lanes are not displaying flashing red lights or a red cross, then you may change to other lanes when safe to do so. The hard shoulder can be used as a running lane when signs are displayed.

Lanes may be closed for different reasons, possibly an accident or breakdown etc.

51. If someone is reversing off a driveway, sound your horn and be prepared to stop.

CASE STUDY

Sara is dropping her children off at their school before driving through residential streets to her office. The streets are in a 20 mph zone and also have road humps and narrowing's. She carefully passes a cyclist as she approaches the school, then parks away from zig-zag lines to let her children out of the car. As she drives away to her office she notices a disabled scooter being driven along on the opposite side of the road.

Q.1. What are road humps and narrowing's on roads known as?
Mark one answer.

a. Traffic restriction measures.
b. Traffic calming measures.
c. Traffic controlling measures.
d. Obstruction routes.

Q.2. Why does she pass the cyclist carefully?
Mark one answer.

a. She is not sure where the cyclist is going.
b. She is frightened of cyclists.
c. The cyclist may wobble or swerve.
d. Cyclists do not consider traffic.

Q.3. Why does Sara park away from the zig-zag lines near the school?
Mark one answer.

a. Because she can't get parked near the school for traffic.
b. Because she knows she would be breaking the law and restricting visibility if she parks on them.
c. Because she likes her children to walk up the road to school for the exercise.
d. She can get to her office quicker from there.

Q.4. What speed limit can a disabled scooter not exceed?
Mark one answer.

a. 12mph.
b. 8mph.
c. 10mph.
d. 6mph.

Chapter 6

OTHER VULNERABLE ROAD USERS

1. Anti-dazzle (mirrors).

If a vehicle is following with the main beam on, the driver in front when checking the mirror can be blinded/dazzled by the vehicle's lights following. To counteract this the interior mirror can be adjusted to the antidazzle position, the mirror is then darker and the lights behind no longer dazzle the driver in front.

2. Do not overtake cycles, motorbikes and mopeds then turn left immediately after.

Rule 182: Do not cut in on cyclists

The driver should stay behind the cyclist until the junction.

3. Never wave children across or into the road.

4. Take more training after passing your test - such as the Pass Plus. This will help to improve your driving skills and reduce risks of collisions. Pass Plus is not available in Northern Ireland.

5. Cyclists, mopeds, motorbikes and pedestrians are more at risk at junctions.

Rule 163: Give vulnerable road users at least as much space as you would a car

Rule 170: Give way to pedestrians who have started to cross

6. Give horse riders and cyclists plenty of room when passing, horses frighten easily and cyclists may need to swerve. They may use the left lane when turning right at roundabouts.

Horses can frighten easily in traffic and panic and cyclists may swerve to avoid hazards such as drains, potholes etc., or be caught by crosswinds and wobble. Cycles and lorries may use a different course when turning right at a roundabout. Cyclists and horse riders because they are more vulnerable may use the left lane when turning right. Lorries or long vehicles may use the left lane when turning right as they need more room to manoeuvre. Slow down and be ready to stop.

7. When reversing if you cannot see clearly, ask someone to guide you or get out and check.

8. Red triangle signs warn motorists of something ahead.

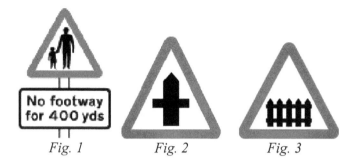

Fig. 1   Fig. 2   Fig. 3

Fig. 1 warns of pedestrians in the road for the distance shown. Fig. 2 denotes a crossroads, the broader line indicates priority through the junction. Fig. 3 shows a level crossing with gate or barrier.

Fig. 4   Fig. 5   Fig. 6

Fig. 7

Fig. 4 indicates a level crossing without gate or barrier. Fig. 5 shows children going to or from school. Fig. 6 indicates a cycle route crossing or joining the road ahead. Fig. 7 shows elderly people crossing.

9. Elderly drivers may have slow reactions and may misjudge your speed.

10. Be patient with learner drivers, they may make mistakes.

11. Motorcyclists should check over their shoulder to check their blind area before turning right.

12. Children are difficult to see when you are reversing.

13. On country roads, pedestrians may walk along the road where there is no pavement.

14. On organised marches people may wear reflective clothing and carry a red light.

If marches or demonstrations are organised properly, safety should be a priority. On organised marches people may wear reflective clothing. If marching at night, they may also carry red lights to warn traffic behind.

15. Motorcyclists may wear bright clothing to be seen more easily.

16. Before turning right, check your right mirror for traffic overtaking.

17. Motorcyclists may use a dipped headlight in daylight to be seen more easily.

18. Motorcycles may swerve around holes, uneven roads, drains etc. Allow them more room.

Motorcycles and cycles may swerve around holes, uneven roads, drains etc., all of which could be hazards for the rider. Motorcycles and cycles may slip on drain covers. Allow plenty room if driving behind them. In slow moving queues of traffic motorcycles may filter through. Be aware when changing lanes.

19. Disabled scooters/powered vehicles may have a flashing amber light/beacon and are not permitted to travel above the limit of 8mph. Also slow moving vehicles may have flashing amber beacons. Mobility scooters travel more slowly than other traffic and may be less visible. They must use lights to be seen at night.

20. Motorcyclists are small and difficult to see at junctions.

21. Do not park on zig-zag lines outside of schools. Children need a clear view of the crossing area.

22. Slow moving vehicles may use flashing amber beacons.

23. Give way to pedestrians that are crossing the road.

Rule 170: Give way to pedestrians who have started to cross

24. In queues of traffic check for motorcycles filtering through on either side.

25. On a Pelican crossing give way to pedestrians when the amber light is flashing. If the crossing is clear you may continue.

26. Warning cycle route ahead.

27. With-flow cycle route.

A with-flow cycle route has both traffic and cycles travelling in the same direction.

28. Shared route for pedestrians and pedal cycles only.

29. Advanced warning line.

Advanced warning lines can be found at traffic lights. These are to protect cyclists. Vehicles cannot enter the area marked with the cycle, traffic must wait behind the advanced warning line. When lights change to green allow the cyclists to move away first. This red area allows cyclists to position in front of traffic.

30. Yellow bar markings on the approach to a roundabout.

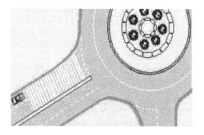

Some roundabouts have yellow bar markings on the approach, other colours are also used. These become closer together the nearer to the roundabout and provide a warning to drivers to slow down.

31. Deaf blind stick.

Blind people may carry a white stick. If a person is both deaf and blind the white stick will also have a red band.

32. A hearing dog for the deaf will wear a burgundy coat signifying that the person they are with is deaf.

If they also have a guide dog it may be wearing a red and white harness.

NORMAL TRAFFIC LIGHTS

Normal sequence is RED - then RED & AMBER showing at the same time - then GREEN - then AMBER - then RED. On a green traffic light, go if it is safe to do so, if the exit to the junction is blocked then do not proceed. On the amber, red or red/amber you must stop at white line if safe to do so.

TRAFFIC LIGHT CROSSINGS

The **PUFFIN, TOUCAN & PEGASUS** Traffic lights have the same system as normal traffic lights. The only different one is the **PELICAN** which has a sequence RED – then FLASHING AMBER – then GREEN - then AMBER - then RED. A green filter arrow is for traffic filtering through in that direction. Do not enter this lane unless you want to go in the direction of the arrow. You can drive on when the green arrow is lit. Give other traffic especially cyclists more room and time to get into the correct lane. Cyclists should wheel their cycles across Pelican, Equestrian,

Puffin or Zebra crossings, they should never ride across. They are allowed to ride across Toucan crossings.

33. Pelican crossings.

PELICAN

A Pelican crossing stands for Pedestrian Electronically Light Controlled - it is controlled by the pedestrian by pushing the button on the box, this will activate the light system. The pedestrian will see a non-flashing RED man while the driver will see a GREEN light. When the system is activated, the GREEN light the driver sees will change to AMBER then RED. At this point the RED man the pedestrian sees will change to a non-flashing GREEN man. After a time, the non-flashing will change to a flashing GREEN man.

At the same time the driver's RED light will change to a flashing AMBER. This indicates that pedestrians are not allowed to start to cross the road, but pedestrians already crossing may continue. The driver must wait if pedestrians are still crossing - if the crossing is clear the driver may continue. The lights will then change again- the pedestrian light back to a static RED light, the drivers light will change to GREEN.

34. Toucan crossings.

TOUCAN

The Toucan crossing stands for Two Can Cross, this refers to pedestrians and cyclists crossing together. On this crossing the pedestrian will see a man and a cycle, operating the same way as a Puffin, the pedestrian or cyclist will need to press a button. Cyclists may ride across Toucans whereas they should dismount at other crossings. There are NO flashing lights.

35. Puffin crossings.

PUFFIN

The Puffin crossing stands for Pedestrian User Friendly Intelligent, it is intelligent because it senses pedestrians. The crossing time is varied depending on the needs of the pedestrian. So the GREEN man will stay on for the pedestrian to clear the crossing. The RED light for the driver will stay on until the pedestrian has cleared the crossing - there are NO flashing lights unlike the Pelican. To activate the system, the pedestrian will press a button.

36. Pegasus crossing (equestrian)

PEGASUS CROSSINGS (EQUESTRIAN)

These are found where a public highway crosses a road and in most cases there will also be a parallel pedestrian or Toucan crossing. The signals for a Pegasus crossing use a ridden horse symbol which shows either RED or GREEN. They are operated the same way as a Toucan by pressing a button.

37. Zebra crossing

ZEBRA

This crossing will have continuous flashing AMBER beacons and is marked by BLACK and WHITE stripes on the road. Pedestrians should never cross the road within the zig-zag areas and drivers should not park on the zig-zag lines or go over the broken line. In queuing traffic, you must keep the zebra crossing clear – do not queue over the crossing. A zebra crossing with a central island is two separate crossings.

38. Watch out for pedestrians leaving buses and crossing the road as they are more vulnerable.

39. When passing sheep, go slowly and allow plenty of room.

40. Flashing amber school sign. Reduce your speed until clear of the area.

41. School bus sign.

42. A school crossing patrol will display a sign to stop traffic.

CASE STUDY

Paul has recently passed his driving test and has bought a car. He is about to start his Pass Plus lessons later in the day. He is driving to college for the first time, as he approaches a roundabout he notices yellow bar markings painted on the road. At the roundabout there is a cyclist in front of him in the left hand lane, he watches to see where the cyclist is heading as he makes his manoeuvre. He follows a learner driver along the road leading to the college car park, the learner driver makes a serious mistake and nearly crashes into Paul's car.

Q.1. What are the benefits of the Pass Plus scheme?
Mark one answer.

a. It helps your car to pass its M.O.T.
b. It improves your driving skills and reduces risks of collisions.
c. It can help you get a job in driving.
d. It helps you drive faster.

Q.2. What do yellow bar markings leading to a roundabout mean?
Mark one answer.

a. They provide a warning to drivers to slow down approaching the roundabout.
b. They point the way to the roundabout.
c. They improve the appearance of the roundabout.
d. They warn of road works.

Q.3. Why is Paul being observant about where the cyclist is heading?
Mark one answer.

a. He doesn't want to travel in the same direction.
b. Paul knows the cyclist may take a different course on the roundabout because he is more vulnerable.
c. He wants to know what type of cycle he is riding.
d. Cyclists never signal.

Q.4. What should Paul do when the learner makes the error.
Mark one answer.

a. Use his horn.
b. Shout at the learner driver.
c. Ignore the drivers error and stay calm.
d. Speed past the learner.

Chapter 7

DIFFERENT TYPES OF VEHICLE

1. Allow cyclists more room when overtaking, they may wobble or swerve unexpectedly and may fall off.

2. In crosswinds the most at risk are; cyclists, high-sided vehicles, motorcyclists.

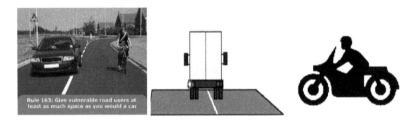

The least at risk in crosswinds are cars.

3. Do not overtake when at or approaching a junction.

Do not overtake cycles or motorcyclists then turn left immediately afterwards, the driver should stay behind the cyclists until after the junction.

4. Class 3 powered vehicles (disabled) maximum speed 8 mph. Mobility scooters travel more slowly than other traffic and may be less visible. They must use lights to be seen at night.

5. Trams cannot steer so be aware.

Electric trams cannot steer, they run on tracks so cannot move out of the way. Signs warn of a tramway route.

6. When overtaking a lorry, remember it takes more time to pass as they are long vehicles. Do not overtake if in doubt, stay well back.

When you are overtaking a lorry make sure you have enough time to overtake and return back to left so as not to endanger yourself or oncoming traffic.

7. Extended-arm side mirrors can be used when towing caravans.

8. Use dipped headlights in bad weather e.g. in darkness, roads with surface spray, poor visibility.

9. Use fog lights if visibility is below 100 metres.

10. Be careful when emerging from junctions especially when lorries are approaching from the right, they can hide overtaking vehicles and motorbikes.

Rule 211: Look out for motorcyclists and cyclists at junctions

Before overtaking large vehicles keep well back for a better view of the road.

11. If you are emerging from a junction in traffic and there are lorries or large vehicles approaching from the right, be extra careful as their size can hide overtaking cars and motorbikes.

12. In windy weather allow extra room when overtaking motorcycles.

13. If spray makes it difficult to see, drop back to increase visibility. Use dipped headlights, if visibility is less than 100 metres, use rear fog lights.

14. Be careful when approaching a stationary bus as it may pull out or pedestrians may walk out from behind.

15. The greatest advantage of a 4-wheel drive vehicle is that it will have additional grip on road surfaces.

16. Give large vehicles room to manoeuvre around corners or at junctions, they may need more room to turn (lorry turning circle). If need be, stay well back to allow them to turn.

17. When following another vehicle, if someone overtakes and fills the gap, drop back further and stay calm.

CASE STUDY

Zara is driving to her parents to take them on holiday, she is towing a caravan. The weather is poor. As she sets off it becomes foggy. She decides she needs her fog lights on. After a short while the fog lifts. It then starts to rain. She is following traffic and because of the wet roads, spray is created from the traffic in front.

Q.1. Which is the best mirror to use when towing her caravan?
Mark one answer.

a. Interior mirror.
b. Extended-arm side mirror.
c. Wing mirror.
d. Vanity mirror.

Q.2. In crosswinds who is least at risk?
Mark one answer.

a. Motorcyclists.
b. Cars.
c. High-sided vehicles.
d. Cyclists.

Q.3. Zara put her fog lights on because of poor visibility, her visibility would have dropped below what?
Mark one answer.

a. 50 metres.
b. 75 metres.
c. 100 metres.
d. 200 metres.

Q.4. Which lights should Zara have on in the poor weather?
Mark one answer.

a. Side lights.
b. Main beam headlights.
c. Hazard lights.
d. Dipped headlights.

Chapter 8

VEHICLE HANDLING IN ROAD CONDITIONS

1. Coasting means that there is no engine braking, you will have less control over your steering and your car will travel faster.

Coasting or free-wheeling is when a vehicle is being driven with the clutch down or in neutral. This will result in less braking and steering control. E.g. when driving down a steep incline such as on country roads, a lower gear should be used and with the clutch up the lower gear will assist with engine braking. Therefore, the brakes may not be in permanent use and this will prevent them from overheating. If a driver is riding the clutch (driving with the clutch down) e.g. coasting, then the hill will encourage the vehicle to travel faster and a driver may over use the brakes. This can result in the brakes overheating and braking power is reduced. This is known as BRAKE FADE.

2. At night time always use dipped headlights on motorways, even when roads are lit. If you stop on the hard shoulder or break down, switch off your headlights and put side lights on – also use hazard warning lights.

When visibility is reduced because of poor conditions or when light is fading, headlights should be switched on when driving on roads including motorways. See and be seen.

3. If you are dazzled by oncoming headlights, you need to slow down or stop.

When driving, if an oncoming vehicle dazzles you because their lights are too bright, slow down or if necessary stop.

4. It is more difficult to see and be seen in fog. When parked in fog, use your sidelights.

5. Motorcyclists may steer round drain covers in wet weather to avoid slipping or skidding.

6. Gauges are often found on the side verges of country roads to warn drivers of fords or snow depth.

7. Reflective studs are used on motorways.

Fig. 1

Reflective studs are used on motorways to help drivers at night or in poor visibility, they are often known as 'cats eyes'. White studs mark traffic lanes (Fig.1), the left hand side of the carriageway is marked with red studs (Fig.1). Amber studs are found between the central reservation and the carriageway on a motorway.

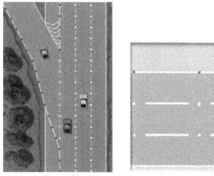

Fig. 2   *Fig. 3*

Green studs are used to mark lay-bys and the entrances to and exits from slip roads (Figs 2 & 3). Yellow/green reflective studs are used for temporary adjustments to lane layouts for motorway maintenance.

8.   Rumble devices are found outside schools, hospitals and at the end of motorways to slow down traffic. They indicate approaching hazards.

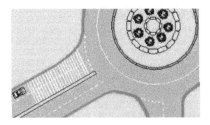

Rumble devices are raised strips across the road to make a driver aware of a potential hazard and encourage them to reduce speed. They make the driver more aware of their speed.

9.   Anti-lock brakes (ABS) on your vehicle reduce the risk of skidding.

Anti-lock brakes (ABS) reduce the risk of skidding if you have to brake in an emergency. If you are driving a vehicle with ABS, apply the foot brake rapidly and firmly. Do not release the brake pedal until you have stopped. ABS does not reduce your stopping distance but you can continue to steer while braking, because the wheels will not lock. ABS will come into effect when the wheels are about to lock. If a car does not have anti-lock braking (ABS) and the car starts to skid, it means the wheels are locking. In this situation the first thing you must do is to release the foot brake then immediately brake again.

10. Trams only allowed.

11. Yellow box junctions.

*Yellow box junctions are used where stationary traffic is likely to block the junction. You **must not** enter the box unless your exit is clear. If you are turning right at the junction you can move into the box and wait for a gap in oncoming traffic but only if the right turn exit is clear.*

12. Chains on tyres help prevent skidding in deep snow.

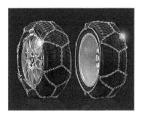

13. Passing places are used on narrow country roads so vehicles can pass safely.

Fig 1.   Fig. 2   Fig. 3

Passing places can be found on very narrow roads e.g. single track roads. As in Fig. 1 when traffic meet on roads like these and they cannot proceed, one vehicle must give way. When driving along, if the passing place is on the left then the driver should pull in to the left to allow the oncoming traffic through. If the passing place is on the right, then the driver should wait opposite the passing place to allow the oncoming traffic through.

14. When driving through a ford, use a low gear and drive slowly, use the brakes afterwards to help dry them and to make sure they work as the brakes will be soaking wet. There may be a depth gauge to judge the depth of the water.

15. Brake fade is when the brakes overheat because they have been used continuously.

16. When driving in fog leave plenty time for your journey, see and be seen and make sure your headlights work and your windows are clean. Rear fog lights make your brake lights less clear to other motorists so be sure to switch them off when visibility improves. Some cars are fitted with front fog lights so remember to switch these off when visibility improves.

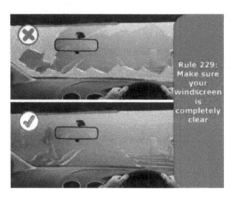

17. If your vehicle goes into a rear wheel skid, steer into it.

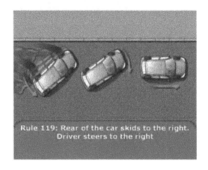

18. Use fog lights when visibility is less than 100 metres, this makes you more visible in fog, then switch them off when visibility improves as they may dazzle other drivers. Driving in clear conditions with fog lights on is illegal.

19. You are allowed to overtake on left;
    a. In one way systems.
    b. When the vehicle in front is turning right.
    c. In slow moving queues.

20. In good dry weather keep a 2 second gap from the car in front.

21. In wet weather double to a 4 second gap behind the car in front.

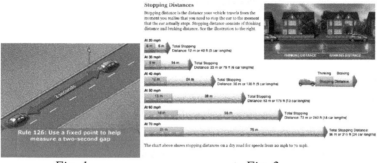

Fig. 1   Fig. 2

You must allow yourself enough time to stop in wet weather.

STOPPING DISTANCES IN FEET

SPEED MPH	THINKING DISTANCE	BRAKING DISTANCE	OVERALL S D SHORTEST S D MINIMUM S D
20 X 2	20	20	40
30 X 2.5	30	45	75
40 X 3	40	80	118
50 X 3.5	50	125	175
60 X 4	60	180	240
70 X 4.5	70	245	315

The table shows the stopping distances in feet. The stopping/braking distance can be worked out by multiplying but this can only be done in feet not metres. The first column shows the speed the vehicle is travelling. The second column shows the thinking distance. The third column shows the braking distance. The fourth column shows the overall/shortest/minimum

81

stopping distance. The thinking distance is always the same in feet as the speed being travelled. The stopping distances in column 4 can be worked out by multiplying by 2 at 20mph. Then increase by a half every 10mph increased.

22. When braking on ice the stopping distance can be 10 times the normal stopping distance. The above calculations work on all distances accurately except the shorter stopping distance at 40mph, this will be 118.

23. In heavy snow only drive if it is essential.

24. Do not overtake approaching bends, at night be more careful as it is more difficult to see.

25. Areas reserved for trams may have white line markings, a different coloured surface and a different surface texture.

*You **MUST NOT** enter a road, lane or other route reserved for trams. Take extra care where trams run along the road. You should avoid driving directly on top of the rails and should take care where trams leave the main carriageway to enter the reserved route, to ensure you do not follow them. The width taken up by trams is often shown by tram lanes marked by white lines, yellow dots or by a different type of road surface. Diamond-shaped signs and white light signals give instructions to tram drivers only.*

26. Road humps for half a mile (distance over which road humps extend). Traffic calming measures are used to slow traffic down, keep a reduced speed throughout.

27. Electronic Stability Control. (ESC).

Electronic Stability Control (ESC) is also referred to as Electronic Stability Program (ESP) or Dynamic Stability Control (DSC). It is a computerized technology that improves the safety of a vehicle's stability when necessary regardless of the road surface or tyre grip. As soon as the vehicle begins to swerve then engine output is reduced and the wheels are braked individually. This increases the driving stability of the vehicle on slippery road surfaces. ESC automatically intervenes to stop a car skidding. According to several agencies loss of life could be prevented by the use of the technology. ESC is now mandatory for all new cars.

28. When driving uphill you may need a lower gear to maintain your speed, the engine will work harder and the hill may make you slow down.

29. Beware of sudden gusts when overtaking vehicles in windy conditions.

30. Different factors can add to the time it takes to stop. These include the weather, the tyres, the speed you are travelling, the road surfaces etc.

CASE STUDY

Colin is driving through countryside in the early evening, the roads are very narrow as at times it becomes a single track. He often has to stop to allow cars approaching to proceed. There are small areas on either side of the road at intervals where they are off the road. He has his dipped headlights on and is careful when he sees an oncoming vehicle in case he has to stop. He changes to a lower gear when he starts to drive down a steep incline and at times needs to reduce his speed on the sharp bends.

Q.1. What are the areas on the sides of the road Colin may use to let other drivers pass?
Mark one answer.

a. Side roads.
b. Passing Places.
c. Hard shoulder.
d. Lay-bys.

Q.2. Why has Colin switched his headlights on in the early evening?
Mark one answer.

a. To check the headlight bulbs.
b. He forgot to check if the headlights were working properly.
c. His visibility is reduced because of the fading light.
d. He is unsure of the country roads.

Q.3. What should Colin expect to see coming towards him on his side of the country roads?
Mark one answer.

a. Horses.
b. Cars.
c. Cycles.
d. Pedestrians.

Q.4. At times Colin changes to a lower gear when travelling down a steep incline. Why does he do this?
Mark one answer.

a. To use the engine as a brake.
b. To avoid skidding.
c. To avoid swerving.
d. To save petrol.

Chapter 9

KNOWING THE RULES OF MOTORWAYS

1. You can use the right hand lane (lane 3) on a 3 lane motorway for overtaking or when there is lane closures or if directed by Police or Highway Agency patrols.

2. If no speed limit signs show, the maximum speed limit on a motorway is 70mph (national speed limit).

3. All lanes on a motorway have a maximum speed of 70mph unless road signs say otherwise. No lane is faster than another.

4. The left lane (lane 1) on a motorway is used for normal driving.

5. When you join a motorway, keep to left lane to build up your speed and have time to adjust to the traffic flow and faster speeds.

6. Motorway phones are normally linked to the police, some areas are now linked to the Highways Agency control centre.

*If your vehicle develops a problem, leave the motorway at the next exit or pull into a service area. If you cannot do so, you should pull on to the hard shoulder and stop as far to the left as possible, with your wheels turned to the left and try to stop near an emergency telephone (situated at approximately one mile intervals along the hard shoulder). Leave the vehicle by the left-hand door and ensure your passengers do the same. You **MUST** leave any animals in the vehicle or, in an emergency, keep them under proper control on the verge. Never attempt to place a warning triangle on a motorway. Do not put yourself in danger by attempting even simple repairs. Ensure that passengers keep away from the carriageway and hard shoulder, and that children are kept under control. Walk to an emergency telephone on your side of the carriageway – the telephone is free of charge and connects directly to the Highways Agency or the Police. Always face the traffic when you speak on the phone and give full details to the Highways Agency or the Police; also inform them if you are a vulnerable motorist such as disabled, older or travelling alone. Then return and wait near your vehicle (well away from the carriageway and hard shoulder). If you feel at risk from another person, return to your vehicle by a left-hand door and lock all doors. Leave your vehicle again as soon as you feel this danger has passed.*

7. A red x on a motorway means - do not continue in that lane. You must obey flashing red lights, these also tell you not to continue. If other lanes are not displaying flashing red lights or a red cross, then you may change to other lanes when safe to do so. The hard shoulder can be used as a running lane when signs are displayed.

Lanes may be closed for different reasons, possibly an accident or breakdown etc.

8. The following are **not allowed** on the motorway;

    a. Learner car drivers e.g.(provisional licence holders).
    b. Horse riders.
    c. Tractors.
    d. Cyclists.
    e. Pedestrians.
    f. Mobility scooters.
    g. Motor cycles under 50cc.

9. If you breakdown on a motorway, find a motorway phone and give the number of the phone you are using.

    Then tell the operator if you are a member of a breakdown organisation i.e. RAC, AA, Green Flag. Give the details of your vehicle. If you are using a mobile phone, give your location from the marker posts, these are 100 metres apart. The picture shows marker posts on the left.

By giving information that you are a member of a breakdown organisation, this could stop the police etc. from wasting their resources. If the problem is not serious they may contact the breakdown company on your behalf therefore avoiding having to send out one of their own patrols. Using an emergency phone assists services to locate you and your vehicle.

10. When driving in a contra-flow system, keep your distance from the car ahead. You may find lower speed limit signs displayed.

11. Emergency refuges are for breakdown only or if directed onto by Police or Highways Agency officers.

An emergency refuge area

12. You must not reverse on a motorway or cross the central reservation. Do not drive against the traffic flow. If you have missed your exit, or have taken the wrong route, carry on to the next exit.

13. The advantage of travelling at a constant speed is that traffic will keep flowing and journey times will improve.

14. Learner car drivers with provisional licenses are **not allowed** on motorways and must be supervised while driving.

15. Traffic joining from a slip road should adjust speed to join in with the traffic on the main carriageway. Sometimes they may have to slow down but most times would normally build speed before joining. **Always** give way to traffic on motorways.

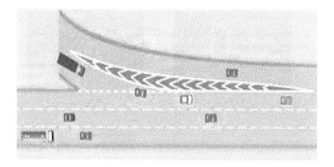

When joining a motorway from a slip road (acceleration lane) you would build speed in the slip road then join the left lane of the carriageway. In the picture the red car joining in the slip road on the left would build speed.

16. After a breakdown use the hard shoulder to build speed before re-joining the motorway/carriageway.

17. Variable speed limits can reduce traffic bunching.

Congestion or traffic bunching is when traffic is building up and sometimes driving too close e.g. tailgating on a motorway.

18. Variable speed limit signs are found in Active Traffic Management areas. When an ATM is in operation all speed limit and direction signs are set.

Fig. 1   *Fig. 2*

Fig. 3   *Fig. 4*

Fig. 5

Active Traffic Management (ATM) Figs 1-5. Consists of traffic monitoring, CCTV camera's watch for accidents happening on motorways. Active traffic management deals with;
Accident control.
Different/variable message signs.
Controlling lane signals.
Variable/different speed limit signs.
Information for drivers.
History of what has happened ahead e.g. incidents or accidents.

19. If you drive at continuous high speeds it will increase the risk of breakdowns because your car is working harder.

Check your vehicle before a long journey to reduce the risk of breakdowns, it is also wise to plan regular rest stops

20. Countdown markers.

Countdown markers indicate the distance to the start of the deceleration lane (to exit the motorway). Each bar represents 100 yards.

21. The left lane on a motorway can be used by any vehicle.

22. When you use the emergency phone on a motorway, face the oncoming traffic. This allows you to see other hazards such as large lorries approaching you. Pedestrians should not be on motorways or slip roads except in emergency situations.

23. The speed limit on motorway when towing a trailer is 60mph.

	Built-up area	Single carriageway	Dual carriageway	Motorway
Cars and Motorcycles	30	60	70	70
Cars towing caravans or trailers	30	50	60	60
Buses and coaches	30	50	60	70
Goods Vehicles * 60 if articulated or towing a trailer	30	50	60	70*
Goods Vehicles exceeding 7.5 tonnes max laden weight	30	40	50	60

24. The overtaking lane on a motorway is the right hand lane, after overtaking always return back to the left as soon as it is safe to do so.

25. Towing is not allowed in the right hand lane of a 3 lane motorway.

26. If you get a flat tyre on a motorway, use an emergency phone and contact the Police or Highways Services Agency for help. Do not try and repair it yourself without assistance.

27. Reflective studs on motorways.

Rule 132: Reflective road studs mark the lanes and edges of the carriageway

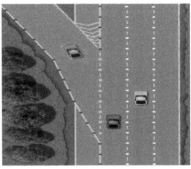

Reflective studs are used on motorways to help drivers at night or in poor visibility, they are often known as 'cat's eyes'. White studs mark traffic lanes, the left hand side of the carriageway is marked with red studs, and amber studs are found between the central reservation and the carriageway on a motorway. Green studs are used to mark lay-bys and the entrances to, and exits from, slip roads. Yellow/green reflective studs are used for temporary adjustments to lane layouts for motorway maintenance.

28. Use hazard lights on your vehicle to warn of hazards ahead or slow moving traffic.

Because traffic travels faster on motorways, if you see a hazard ahead warn traffic behind why you are braking by using the hazard warning lights briefly. This will help them understand that it is not normal braking and hopefully make them ready to reduce speed themselves.

29. Crawler lanes are found on steep gradients on motorways.

30. Buses are allowed on motorways.

31. If you become tired whilst driving on a motorway, turn off at your next exit or pull in at a service area to rest before continuing your journey.

32. If traffic is joining from a slip road when you are travelling on a motorway be prepared to move lanes to allow them to join safely.

33. Highway Agency Officers can stop and direct anyone on a motorway.

CASE STUDY

Tony is driving on a three lane motorway and is towing a trailer. There are road works ahead and a contra-flow system is in place. Tony is driving in heavy traffic in the contra-flow. The road works continue for 3 miles with a speed limit of 40 mph. After the road works clear the speed limit returns to the national speed limit.

Q.1. While driving Tony see red studs on his left and white studs on his right. Which lane is Tony driving in?
Mark one answer.

a. The right lane.
b. The middle lane.
c. The left lane.
d. The hard shoulder.

Q.2. What is the maximum speed Tony is allowed to drive towing his trailer when he sees the national speed limit sign?
Mark one answer.

a. 50 mph.
b. 60 mph.
c. 70 mph.
d. 80 mph.

Q.3. Which lanes can Tony use when towing his trailer?
Mark one answer.

a. Only the left lane.
b. Only the right lane.
c. Only the middle and right lane.
d. Only the middle and left lane.

Q.4. What is the hard shoulder on the motorway for?
Mark one answer.

a. Overtaking.
b. Parking.
c. Resting.
d. Breakdowns and emergencies.

Chapter 10

KNOWING THE RULES OF THE ROAD

1. Rules of flashing amber on a pelican crossing, give way to pedestrians on the crossing.

PELICAN

A Pelican crossing stands for Pedestrian Electronically Light Controlled - it is controlled by the pedestrian by pushing the button on the box, this will activate the light system. The pedestrian will see non-flashing RED man while the driver will see a GREEN light. When the system is activated, the GREEN light the driver sees will change to AMBER then RED. At this point the RED man the pedestrian sees will change to a non-flashing GREEN man. After a time, the non-flashing will change to a flashing GREEN man. At the same time the driver's RED light will change to a flashing AMBER. This indicates that pedestrians are not allowed to start crossing the road, but pedestrians already crossing may continue. The driver must wait if pedestrians are still crossing, if the crossing is clear the driver may continue. The lights will then change again - the pedestrian light back to a static RED light, the driver's light will change to GREEN.

2. Meter Zone (here you pay to park with waiting restrictions) and Zone Ends signs.

3. Concealed level crossing countdown markers. If the red lights continue to flash, keep on waiting.

4. Urban clearway sign; you are not allowed to stop at any time except to set down or pick up passengers. Fig. 1.

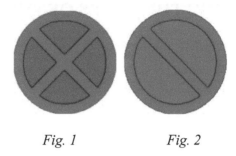

Fig. 1   *Fig. 2*

Fig. 2 Waiting restrictions apply.

An information plate will be nearby possibly on a lamp post to qualify the times allowed to park.

5. You are not allowed to reverse from a side road into a main road.

6. At unmarked crossroads - no-one has priority, proceed with caution.

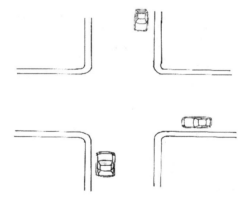

7. Street lighting may indicate there is a 30mph speed limit.

If the speed limit is different e.g. higher - 40mph, 50mph etc., small repeater speed limit signs should be displayed. Where there is a reduced speed limit below 30 mph e.g. 20mph, there may be repeater signs displayed, speed humps, chicanes etc.

8. On a two or three lane dual carriageway, the right lane may be used for overtaking and turning right.

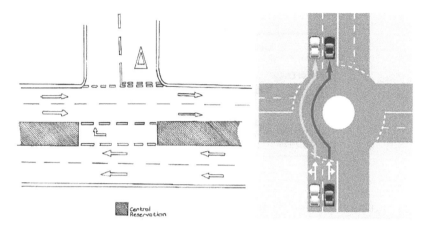

Central Reservation

9. Zone ends.

The sign shows a maximum 20mph zone has ended and you are now entering a maximum 30mph zone.

10. Brake lights are warning signals to other drivers, the same as indicators.

Brake lights warn drivers behind you are slowing down or stopping.

11. When indicating on a roundabout, indicate left after you have passed the exit – before the exit you want, then indicate left before you leave the roundabout.

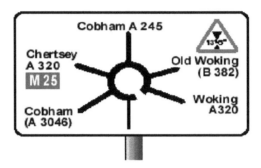

*For example, on the sign if you were travelling straight ahead to the A245 for Cobham, on the approach no signal would be given, you would continue past Cobham A3046 in the left lane unless road markings or signs indicate otherwise. Continue with no signal. Drive past the exit for Chertsey A320, then when past the Chertsey exit but **before** you exit for Cobham, signal left to tell other drivers you are ready to leave the roundabout for Cobham A245. If you wished to drive to Old Woking (B382), you would use the right lane continue round, then signal left **after** you passed the exit for Cobham (A245).*

12. Parking at night time - you are allowed to park on the left or right in a one-way street unless road signs or lines on the road say otherwise. When parking on a road if the speed limit is above 30mph you must use parking lights.

13. Minimum speed and minimum speed ends.

Fig 1   *Fig 2*

The minimum speed you are allowed to drive if you see the sign in Fig.1 is 60mph. You are not allowed to drive at a lower speed if the road is clear. Fig.2 tells you the minimum speed limit has ended.

14. Drivers are only allowed to park in disabled bays if they display a blue badge.

15. 10 metres is the nearest distance you are allowed to park next to a junction (15 metres in Northern Ireland).

16. When reversing, never reverse longer than necessary.

17. When reversing, you are allowed to remove your seat belt.

18. When reversing round a corner, the biggest hazard to other vehicles is when the front of the vehicle swings out.

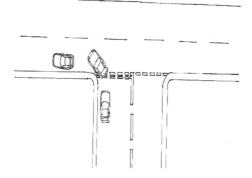

When reversing around a corner, observation and courtesy are important. The biggest hazard to other vehicles is when the front of the vehicle swings out. This can affect oncoming and overtaking traffic. If you are unsure, get out and check or ask someone to guide you round.

19. You can drive across a footpath to access a property.

20. Cyclists, lorries, long vehicles and horse riders may take an unusual route around a roundabout.

Cyclists and horse riders are more vulnerable so may take the left lane when turning right. Long vehicles and lorries may take the left lane when turning right, or may swing out to the right when turning left as they need more room to manoeuvre. Always expect cyclists and horse riders to go in any direction.

21. Turning right at a crossroads. e.g. offside to offside.

When vehicles meet when turning right at a crossroads, where possible and if they have enough room they should turn right offside to offside. The offside is the driver's side.

22. You cannot park; on the brow of a hill, near a bus stop or less than 10 metres from a junction (15 metres in Northern Ireland).

23. Passing places.

Passing places can be found on very narrow roads e.g. single track roads. When traffic meets on a road like this and they cannot proceed, one vehicle must give way. When driving along if the passing place is on the left then the driver should pull into the left to allow the oncoming traffic through as in the pictures shown.

24. Dipped headlights are used to see and be seen.

Dipped headlights are for use at night to see more clearly. They should also be used in bad weather so other motorists can see other traffic more easily. Another time they may be used is in bright sunlight when the sun is low and drivers are dazzled/blinded by the sun e.g. when a driver emerges

at a junction and it is difficult to see because of the sun, if other drivers have their lights on it is easier to see them. Motorcyclists may have a dipped headlight on to be seen more easily even in daylight.

25. Edge of the road line.

The white lines show the edge of the road. This is common where there is no pavement or pathway.

26. Yellow box junction - do not enter the box if your exit is blocked, the exit must be clear.

*Yellow box junctions are used where stationary traffic is likely to block the junction. You **must not** enter the box unless your exit is clear. If you are turning right at the junction you can move into the box and wait for a gap in oncoming traffic but only if the right turn exit is clear.*

27. The speed limit on motorways and dual carriageways is 70mph. Towing trailers or caravans 60mph. The speed limit on single carriageways is 60mph. Towing trailers or caravans 50mph. Fig. 1 shows the national speed limit sign. Fig. 2 shows the speed limits for different vehicles.

	Built-up area	Single carriageway	Dual carriageway	Motorway
Cars and Motorcycles	30	60	70	70
Cars towing caravans or trailers	30	50	60	60
Buses and coaches	30	50	60	70
Goods Vehicles * 60 if articulated or towing a trailer	30	50	60	70*
Goods Vehicles exceeding 7.5 tonnes max laden weight	30	40	50	60

Fig. 1   *Fig. 2*

28. When passing parked cars expect: -

   a. Drivers doors to open.
   b. Vehicles may move off.
   c. Children may run out from behind cars.

29. Be patient at zebra crossings. Allow pedestrians to cross. Do not wave pedestrians across.

Fig. 1

Do not wave pedestrians across as there may be another vehicle approaching. Sign warns you are approaching a zebra crossing Fig. 1.

30. Do not park next to school entrances, or on zig-zag lines on crossings or at bus stops.

 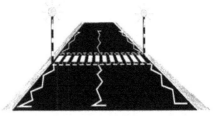

31. When driving over level crossings and warning lights come on, continue and clear the crossing.

When driving over level crossings and the warning lights start to flash (you may also hear an audible warning), carry on clear of the crossing. If you break down on the crossing get everyone out immediately. Contact the signal operator using the emergency phone, do not try to re-start the vehicle unless the operator tells you to.

32. At Toucan crossings both pedestrians & cyclists can cross.

TOUCAN

The Toucan crossing stands for Two Can Cross, this refers to pedestrians and cyclists crossing together. On this crossing the pedestrian will see a man and a cycle, operating the same way as a Puffin, the pedestrian or cyclist will need to press a button. Cyclists may ride across Toucans whereas they should dismount at other crossings. There are NO flashing lights.

33. You must stop when Police, Highway Agency officers, school crossing patrols and red lights tell you to, or in an incident where damage or injury is caused.

34. When driving at night with lights on full/main beam, change back to dipped headlights as soon as another vehicle passes.

When driving at night if driving on an unlit road, you should use main beam headlights also called full beam headlights. You should not use these if following other traffic or traffic is coming towards you. If you are driving with full/main beam lights, switch them off as soon as another overtaking motorist passes so as not to blind them and use dipped headlights.

35. Highway Agency traffic officers can signal you to stop e.g. to control traffic.

36. Turning right across a dual carriageway with a narrow central reservation, make sure the roads are clear in both directions.

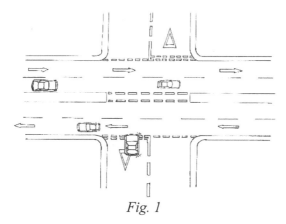

Fig. 1

In Fig. 1 as the central reservation is smaller, you must make sure both approaches from the right and left are clear of traffic and when clear you may drive across in one go as there is not enough room to wait in the central reservation. Waiting in the central reservation would mean the vehicle would be blocking the right hand lane.

37. At night park in well-lit areas for safety and security or park in a garage.

38. High-occupancy lanes (HOV) can be used by vehicles with one or more passengers.

Fig. 1   Fig. 2

Shown in Figs 1 & 2, high-occupancy lanes are similar to bus lanes and can be used by vehicles if there are one or more passengers, including the driver. If there is a requirement for at least two passengers in the vehicle there will be a 3+ car symbol. Solo motorcycles are normally allowed to use HOV lanes but large lorries are likely to be prohibited. The HOV signs indicate which vehicles are permitted in the lane. The aim of a HOV (high occupancy vehicles) lane is to reduce traffic congestion by maximising the use of a bus lane and encourage car sharing.

39. In contra-flow systems on motorways with lane closures, some traffic lanes that remain open may also have restrictions relating to vehicle weight or height.

Fig. 1

As shown in Fig. 1, the right lane closes so traffic will have to move to the left lanes in good time. Traffic in the left lanes will need to be careful of traffic cutting in.

40. You must not stop or park on the carriageway or hard shoulder of a motorway except in an emergency.

41. You must not stop or park near a pedestrian crossing including the area marked by zig-zag lines or on a clearway.

42. Cycle lanes; these are shown by road markings and signs. You **MUST NOT** drive or park in a cycle lane marked by a solid white line during its times of operation. Do not drive or park in a cycle lane marked by a broken white line unless it is unavoidable. You **MUST NOT** park in any cycle lane whilst waiting restrictions apply.

43. If you find you are travelling in the wrong direction, turn around in a side road.

44. In one way streets you may overtake on the left or the right if safe to do so.

45. Give way to oncoming traffic if your side of the road is obstructed.

46. Keep to the left in normal driving.

47. Do not overtake if in doubt.

48. You must not park or stop on a road marked with double white lines or broken line except to pick up and drop off passengers.

49. You may drive a car in this bus lane outside the hours of operation.

50. If you find you are driving in the wrong lane, if road markings are obscured, do not cut across lanes and obstruct other drivers. Continue in that lane and find a safe place to turn round, and rejoin your original route.

CASE STUDY

Ross is driving home alone after college. He exits the college onto the main road and drives along an urban clearway then into the town. There are high-occupancy vehicle lanes (HOV lanes) that Ross does not use. He follows a slow moving council vehicle with a flashing beacon, he then overtakes when it is safe. Ross lives in a one-way street. When he arrives home he finds a safe place to park. He is careful not to park to close to a junction.

Q.1. What colour beacon would the slow moving council vehicle have?
Mark one answer.

a. Green.
b. Red.
c. Amber.
d. White.

Q.2. In the one-way street where can Ross park?
Mark one answer.

a. Only on the left.
b. Only on the right.
c. Either on the right or left.
d. In the centre of the road.

Q.3. Why does Ross not use the high-occupancy vehicle lane?
Mark one answer.

a. It is for vehicles with red flashing beacons.
b. It is for lorries only.
c. It is for vehicles which have two or more occupants.
d. It is for buses only.

Q.4. What is the closest Ross may park next to a junction?
Mark one answer.

a. 5 Metres (10 Metres in Northern Ireland).
b. 10 Metres (15 Metres in Northern Ireland).
c. 15 Metres (20 Metres in Northern Ireland).
d. 20 Metres (25 Metres in Northern Ireland).

Chapter 11

KNOWING YOUR ROAD AND TRAFFIC SIGNS

1. Junction numbers shown on motorway sign.

The junction numbers inform the driver of the numbered exits on the motorway e.g. Junction 25.

2. With-flow and contra-flow.

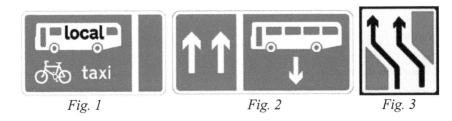

| *Fig. 1* | *Fig. 2* | *Fig. 3* |

Fig. 1 is a with-flow bus, taxi and cycle lane, fig. 2 is a contra-flow bus lane found in one way systems, fig. 3 is a contra-flow, flowing in the same direction found on road works on dual carriageways and motorways etc. It is important to keep a safe separation distance from the vehicle in front and choose the correct lane in plenty of time.

3. Traffic lights not working.

When traffic lights are not working (out of order) proceed with caution. No-one has priority.

4. Hidden dip.

5. Arm signals to be used if indicators on your car are not working. If your signals that you give may be unclear to other drivers, give the appropriate arm signal to confirm.

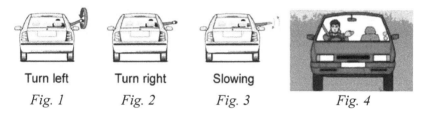

| Turn left | Turn right | Slowing | |
| Fig. 1 | Fig. 2 | Fig. 3 | Fig. 4 |

The use of hand signals would occur if your vehicle has electronic signalling failure or if an indicator bulb fails. There are also situations where hand signals could aid in informing other drivers e.g. in heavily congested areas. Fig. 1 is the hand signal for turning left, fig.2 indicates that you are going to turn right, fig. 3 indicates that you are slowing down e.g. when approaching a zebra crossing. Fig. 4 is not used to inform traffic behind that you are turning left but to inform people in front that you are turning left e.g. traffic controllers or approaching traffic. However, the use of hand signals is rarely seen or used.

6. Crosswinds or side winds sign.

This shows the road sign for side winds also known as crosswinds. These road signs will be in vulnerable areas like open stretches of road, bridges etc.

7. Blue signs usually give mandatory instruction.

Fig. 1   Fig. 2   Fig. 3   Fig. 4   Fig. 5   Fig. 6

*Blue road signs are mandatory (blue **must do**). Fig. 1 means pass on the left side and on the right if the arrow is reversed. Fig. 2 shows the sign which will be used on the back of a road maintenance vehicle indicating that traffic must pass on the left. If both right and left arrows are shown (Fig. 3) this means pass on either side to reach the same destination. The blue 30 fig. 4, means minimum speed, in this case if the road is clear, you cannot drive below 30mph. Fig. 5 shows a one-way street. Fig. 6 means ahead only.*

8. Red triangles indicate warnings.

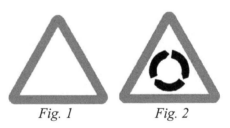

Fig. 1   Fig. 2

Red triangles are a warning of something ahead Fig. 1, Fig. 2 shows a roundabout ahead.

9. Red circles - tell you what you **must not** do.

Fig. 1   Fig. 2   Fig. 3

Red circles tell you that you are not allowed (must not do). Fig. 1 is no overtaking, Fig. 2 is no motor vehicles allowed, Fig. 3 is no cars allowed.

10. Speed limit signs - in a built up area normally 30mph. Do not exceed this speed.

Where there are street lights with no road signs you can generally assume the speed limit is maximum 30mph. If the speed limit is different, then small repeater signs should be displayed, on lamp posts etc.

11. In narrow residential areas speed limits may be reduced to 20mph.

12. National speed limit.

	Built-up area	Single carriageway	Dual carriageway	Motorway
Cars and Motorcycles	30	60	70	70
Cars towing caravans or trailers	30	50	60	60
Buses and coaches	30	50	60	70
Goods Vehicles * 60 if articulated or towing a trailer	30	50	60	70 *
Goods Vehicles exceeding 7.5 tonnes max laden weight	30	40	50	60

Fig. 1   Fig. 2

Fig. 1 is the National Speed limit. Fig. 2 shows the speed limits for various type of vehicles.

13. Yellow box junctions.

Rule 174: Enter a box junction only if your exit road is clear

*Yellow box junctions are used where stationary traffic is likely to block the junction. You **must not** enter the box unless your exit is clear. If you are turn right at the junction you can move into the box and wait for a gap in oncoming traffic but only if the right turn exit is clear.*

14. Passing places.

Passing places can be found on very narrow roads e.g. single track roads. When traffic meets on a road like this and they cannot proceed, one vehicle must give way. When driving along, if the passing place is on the left then the driver should pull in to the left to allow the oncoming traffic through as in the pictures shown. If the passing place is on the right, then the driver should wait opposite to allow the oncoming traffic through the passing place.

15. Studs on motorways.

Rule 132: Reflective road studs mark the lanes and edges of the carriageway

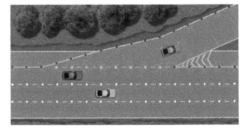

Reflective studs are used on motorways to help drivers at night or in poor visibility, they are often known as 'cats eyes'. White studs mark traffic lanes, the left hand side of the carriageway is marked with red studs and amber studs are found between the central reservation and the carriageway on a motorway. Green studs are used to mark lay-bys, also entrances and exits on slip roads.

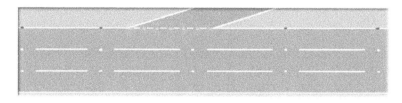

Yellow/green reflective studs are used for temporary adjustments to lane layouts for motorway maintenance.

16.   Traffic lights, order of light changes.

NORMAL TRAFFIC LIGHTS

Normal sequence is RED - then RED & AMBER showing at the same time - then GREEN – then AMBER - then RED. On a green traffic light, go if it safe to do so, if the exit to the junction is blocked then do not proceed. On the amber, red or red/amber you must stop at the white line. A green filter arrow is for traffic filtering through in that direction. Do not enter this lane unless you want to go in the direction of the arrow. You can drive on when the green arrow is lit. Give other traffic especially cyclists more room and time to get into the correct lane. Cyclists should wheel their cycles across Pelican, Equestrian, Puffin or Zebra crossings, they should never ride across. They are allowed to ride across Toucan crossings.

TRAFFIC LIGHT CROSSINGS

The **PUFFIN** & **TOUCAN** *Traffic lights have the same system as normal traffic lights e.g. as above. The only different one is the **PELICAN** which has a sequence RED - then FLASHING AMBER – then GREEN - then AMBER - then RED.*

PELICAN

A pelican crossing stands for Pedestrian Electronically Light Controlled - it is controlled by the pedestrian by pushing the button on the box this will activate the light system. The pedestrian will see a non-flashing RED man while the driver will see a GREEN light. When the system is activated, the GREEN light the driver sees will change to AMBER then RED. At this point the RED man the pedestrian sees will change to a non-flashing GREEN man. After a time, the non-flashing will change to a flashing GREEN man. At the same time the driver's RED light will change to a flashing AMBER. This indicates that pedestrians are not allowed to start to cross the road, but pedestrians already crossing may continue. The driver must wait if pedestrians are still crossing – if the crossing is clear the driver may continue. The lights will then change again- the pedestrian light back to a static RED light, the drivers light will change to GREEN.

17. No entry.

18. Clearway signs mean no waiting and no stopping.

19. Crossroads.

20. Warning - pedestrians walking on road.

This road sign will be displayed where there is no pathway/pavement e.g. on a country road where you may find pedestrians walking towards you on your side of the road.

21. Urban clearway with restricted waiting times.

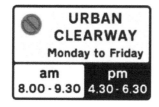

22. Height restrictions.

23. Park and ride.

This road sign, can be found in places where traffic is likely to be deterred/put off from entering city centres, possibly where tolls or

*congestion charges may be in force, so drivers are encouraged to park
their vehicle then use public transport to get to their destination.*

24.   Tourist signs.

*Tourist signs help make drivers aware of tourist spots and places of
interest. The white line in picture 3 shows the edge of the carriageway as
there is no pavement.*

25.   No through road.

26.   Route for trams only (blue). The red triangle sign warns of trams
      crossing the road ahead. The give way sign warns to give way to
      trams.

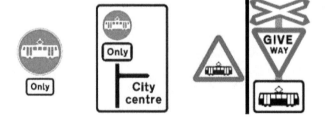

27. End of dual carriageway, two-way traffic straight ahead.

Fig. 1   *Fig. 2*

Fig. 1 shows the dual carriageway ending. Fig. 2 may follow Fig. 1 showing that you will be driving on a carriageway with two-way traffic and traffic may be coming towards you.

28. Give priority to oncoming traffic.

29. Parking 1 mile.

This sign tells you the distance to a parking area.

30. Priority over oncoming traffic.

31. Mandatory instruction blue sign.

Blue circle signs are mandatory and indicate that you 'must do' or 'must obey'.

32. Stop sign.

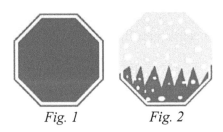

Fig. 1   Fig. 2

Fig. 1 shows a stop sign. A driver must stop at this sign before proceeding even if the road is clear. This sign is unique as it stands out because of its shape. If snow is falling and the sign is covered, it is easy to distinguish it. Fig. 2.

33. Road markings.

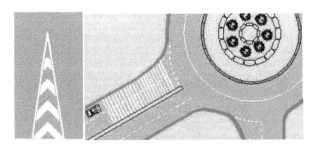

Fig. 1   Fig. 2

Fig. 1 shows chevron markings which are used on carriageways where the traffic passes in the same direction on either side. The continuous boundary line means that vehicles must not enter the area unless there is an emergency. Fig. 2, these markings are used on the approach to roundabouts to alert drivers to a hazard ahead and encourages them to reduce speed.

34. Drivers can cross the solid centre line when overtaking vehicles travelling 10mph or less.

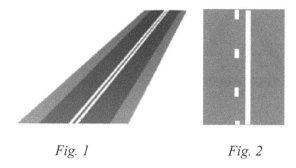

Fig. 1   Fig. 2

Fig. 1 warns drivers cannot cross the solid white line. They may only cross the line if overtaking a vehicle travelling at 10 mph or less. In fig. 2 where the line is broken, drivers may cross the broken line on their side when overtaking if it is safe to do so.

35. Zone ends.

Fig. 1   Fig. 2

Zone Ends – Fig. 1 indicates where a particular zone ends (waiting restrictions ended) and shows you are leaving a controlled restricted parking zone. The restrictions have ended e.g. zone ends. Fig. 2 shows the 20 mph speed limit zone has ended and you are entering a 30mph speed limit zone.

36. Ford.

Fig. 1   *Fig. 2*

Fig. 1 shows a red triangle sign used to warn drivers that they are approaching a ford (a dip in the road which fills with water) sometimes this is accompanied by a depth gauge to warn of the water depth, Fig. 2.

37. Downwards steep hill.

This is another warning sign that there is a steep downward hill ahead, the percentage indicates the steepness. The sign reversed indicates an uphill gradient.

38. Keep left arrow.

This sign tells drivers to pass on the left.

39. Hazard warning line, centre line.

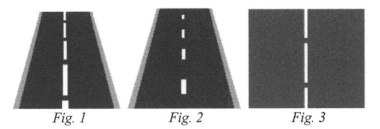

Fig. 1   *Fig. 2*   *Fig. 3*

Fig. 1 shows the centre hazard line on a single carriageway road. Fig. 2

shows the centre line separating traffic on a single carriageway. Fig. 3
shows a hazard warning line (which replaces the centre line or lane line)
an upright sign may indicate the hazard ahead i.e. a bend in the road.
This line is also used on the approach to a junction. A good indicator is the
more white paint, the more danger.

40. Level crossing pictures.

| Fig. 1 | Fig. 2 | Fig. 3 |

Fig. 1 is of a level crossing with gate/barrier. These flashing red lights can
also be found at fire stations and lifting bridges. Fig. 2 is a level crossing
with no gate or barrier. Fig. 3 shows the 3 countdown markers you may
see when approaching a concealed level crossing. Each bar denotes 100
yards, these may be found e.g. where the level crossing is round a bend.

41. Ring road.

This sign indicates a Ring Road ahead. A ring road is a road that can skirt
around a city centre to avoid heavy city traffic therefore avoiding stopping
and starting at junctions in busy traffic. A ring road may add distance on
to a journey but in the long run you may arrive at the destination
quicker.

42. Road humps.

| Fig. 1 | Fig. 2 | Fig. 3 |

| *Fig. 4* | *Fig. 5* |

Fig.1 gives an overhead view of the markings on speed humps. Fig. 2 shows a warning triangle on the approach to speed humps. Figs 3-5 are examples of speed humps. These encourage drivers to reduce speed.

43. Diversion sign.

This is an example of a diversion route sign. These come in different shapes i.e. shapes include diamonds, circles, squares etc. In an emergency, when it is necessary to close a section of motorway or other main road to traffic, a temporary sign may advise drivers to follow a diversion route. To help with navigation black symbols on yellow patches may be displayed on existing direction signs, including motorway signs. On all-purpose roads the symbols may be used on separate signs with yellow backgrounds.

44. Trams - must stop.

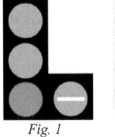 

| *Fig. 1* | *Fig.2* |

Fig. 1 is a set of traffic lights controlling traffic and trams. Here it shows trams must stop and traffic may continue on the green light. If the white line is vertical trams may continue. Fig. 2 warns you are approaching a tramway crossing in front.

45. Motorway - right hand lane closed.

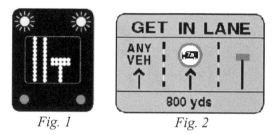

Fig. 1   *Fig. 2*

Fig. 1 is a motorway sign showing the right-hand lane is closed. Fig. 2 is a roadwork sign.

46. Mini-roundabout sign/road markings. Always give way to the right.

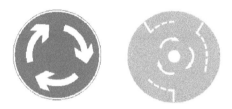

47. Quayside or river bank.

48. Humpback bridge.

49. End of motorway.

50. Roundabout.

51. Danger ahead.

This is a warning sign of a dangerous hazard ahead of you, the sign may be accompanied by an information plate informing you of the danger ahead e.g. pedestrians crossing a high speed road, a hidden dip, falling rocks etc.

52. Give way.

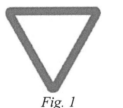

Fig. 1   Fig. 2

Fig. 1 shows an inverted triangle. This is a warning to prepare to give way at a junction. The sign is an inverted triangle (upside down triangle) to stand out. For example, in bad weather i.e. snow, like the stop sign, if covered by snow it is easily seen therefore warning of a junction. Fig. 2 is the same symbol painted on the road on the approach to a junction and approaching a give way sign.

53. Pedestrian emergency exit.

This sign shows the direction to the emergency exit for pedestrians in a road tunnel.

54. End of restriction - motorway sign.

This sign indicates the end of temporary restrictions on a motorway.

55. Zebra crossing ahead.

56. Risk of ice.

57. Two-way traffic crosses one-way road.

This sign indicates that two-way traffic on route crossing ahead. This sign can be found after driving on a one-way street approaching the ends of the road e.g. two-way traffic crosses one-way road.

58. Vehicles may park fully on verge or footpath.

This sign indicates that vehicles may park fully on the verge or footpath e.g. pavement.

59. Crawler lane for heavy or slow vehicles.

Crawler lanes are found on steep gradients. These lanes are for slower traffic and heavy vehicles. They help prevent disruption to the normal traffic flow.

60. Leave the motorway at the next exit.

This sign is used on motorways to indicate to drivers to leave at the next exit, the sign has flashing amber lights. This may be because of a possible accident on the motorway ahead, road repairs etc. and the motorway is closed.

61. Emergency refuge area.

An emergency refuge area

This picture depicts an emergency refuge area found on motorways for vehicles to park safely in emergency situations. These areas can be found in Active Traffic Management areas (ATM) where there is no hard shoulder for emergencies.

62. T junction shows the main through road.

63. Staggered junction.

64. No solo motorcycles.

65. Tunnel sign.

66. Children crossing.

67. Motorway sign for temporary maximum speed limit.

68. Road works speed limit ahead.

Mandatory
speed
limit ahead

69. Motorway lane closed sign.

70. Move to left lane on motorway.

71. Low bridge ahead.

This sign is an advanced warning of a mandatory height restriction ahead; the sign may include an arrow if the restriction is on a side road.

72. Road narrows on both sides.

73. Junction with reduced visibility.

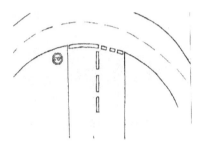

Be careful when emerging at junctions, there is often reduced visibility. Do not pull out of a junction unless you are sure of approaching traffic's intentions e.g. if an approaching vehicle from the right is signalling left make sure they are turning in. Blind junctions also car pillars etc. can make it difficult to see motorcyclists, cyclists etc.

74. Cycle route.

75. Level crossing with gate or barrier.

76. No right turn.

77. Right lane closed.

78. Red hatched markings.

Central hatched markings often coloured red and traffic islands, are used to separate traffic travelling in opposite directions.

79. Turn left ahead.

80. Road narrows on the left.

81. Road narrows on the right.

82. Cycle route joining or crossing road ahead.

83. Double bend ahead.

84. Using your horn is to make people aware of your presence. You must not use your horn between the times of 11.30p.m. and 7a.m. or when stationary unless a moving vehicle may cause you danger.

85. When followed by a police car, if the officer flashes headlights and points to the left, obey and pull up on the left.

86. If you need to pull up after a junction on the left, signal when passing the junction, not before.

87. You may use hazard warning lights briefly on the motorway and dual carriageway to warn of approaching hazards e.g. slow traffic ahead, accidents etc.

88. No parking at any time on the zig zag lines or on the pedestrian crossing. In queuing traffic, you must keep the zebra crossing clear – do not queue over the crossing. A zebra crossing with a central island is two separate crossings.

89. Markings found on motorway slip roads.

90. Police officer stopping traffic.

91. Keep clear markings often found at the entrances to schools.

92. Keep left of hatched markings.

93. The right hand lane (lane 3) in a 3 lane motorway is the overtaking lane.

Refer to **Know Your Traffic Signs** book available from www.tso.co.uk for more information.

CASE STUDY

Chris is driving through an area busy with pedestrians. He sees a turning ahead of him with a red circle sign showing a car with a motorcycle above it. On a stretch of the single carriageway there are double unbroken solid white lines running along the centre. There are several brown upright signs along the road.

Q.1. What is meant by the red circle sign described?
Mark one answer.

a. No motor vehicles.
b. No large vehicles.
c. No vehicle parking.
d. No through road.

Q.2. What do the centre white line markings tell Chris?
Mark one answer.

a. Do not speed.
b. Do not reverse.
c. Do not park.
d. Do not cross the lines.

Q.3. What is the national speed limit for cars and motorcycles on this single carriageway road?
Mark one answer

a. 60mph.
b. 70mph.
c. 40mph.
d. 50mph.

Q.4. What details would Chris find on the brown signs?
Mark one answer.

a. Cyclist information.
b. Weather information.
c. Tourist information.
d. Safety information.

Chapter 12

RELEVANT DRIVING DOCUMENTS

1. Driving Vehicles Licensing Agency. (D.V.L.A.)

The DVLA maintains the register of drivers and vehicles in Great Britain. This information assists in improving road safety, reduces vehicle related crime, supports environmental initiatives and limits vehicle tax evasion.

2. The Driving Standards Agency. (D.S.A.)

The DSA changed to DVSA (see note 3 below) and exists to improve road safety in Great Britain by setting standards for driving and motorcycling and for the education and training of drivers and riders. They also carry out theory and practical driving tests and riding tests.

3. Vehicle and Operator Services Agency. (V.O.S.A.)

VOSA/DVSA improve road safety by ensuring drivers, vehicle operators and M.O.T. garages understand and comply with road worthiness standards. They also provide a range of vehicle licensing, testing and enforcement services. They merged with the DSA to become the DVSA (Driving and Vehicle Standards Agency) in 2014.

4. Vehicle insurance.

    a. Insurance cover note - temporary cover before you receive the full insurance certificate.

An insurance cover note is proof of insurance. A cover note is a temporary document as the full policy can take time to be issued. Therefore, if proof of insurance is needed by police etc., the cover note can be issued by an insurance broker/agent. Depending on the insurer used, the cover note can cover for a maximum of 60 days.

    b. Insurance excess.

The excess on insurance cover is the amount the customer pays in the event of a claim. For example, if a driver has an accident and it is their fault or non-fault, the insurance company can ask for that amount first. If someone has a low excess the cost of the insurance may be more expensive.

If it is a high excess the insurance may be cheaper. So if a person's excess is £200 the full insurance may be £1,000. In the event of a claim the customer would pay the first £200 of any repairs. If the excess was £300 the total insurance payable may be reduced to a lower sum e.g. £800 and in the event of an accident the first £300 would need to be paid. If it was a non-fault accident, then the excess could be claimed back from the third party (the other driver).

    c. Minimum insurance needed is third party.

Minimum insurance allowed by law is third party. This, like all insurance, cover other people injured and damage to their property. It would not pay for repair or damage to the policy holder's own car or property etc. if it was their fault.

    d. Full insurance cover is comprehensive.

Comprehensive insurance protects the third party plus the policy holder's property e.g. car, if it was the policy holder's fault.

    e. Personal injury insurance to cover you for accidents.

Personal accident policies cover only the person insured.

5.   Vehicle Registration (V5C) also known as the log book. You must update this when: -

    a. You move house/change address.
    b. You change your name i.e. marry.
    c. You change the vehicle.
    d. You change any information.

6. Statutory Off Road Notification (SORN). This is valid for 12 months or until the vehicle is taxed, sold or scrapped and informs the D.V.L.A. that the vehicle is not being used on the road. (Fig 1.)

Fig. 1

7. Pass Plus: -

    a. Will improve your knowledge on roads and motorways.
    b. Improve your basic skills.
    c. Will widen your driving experience.
    d. It may reduce your car insurance
    (This scheme is not available in Northern Ireland)

Pass Plus is a course given by a Driving Instructor after a pupil passes a driving test. It consists of a minimum of 6 hours' tuition to improve the driving skills of a pupil.

The course covers: -

1. Town driving.
2. All weather driving.
3. Out of town driving and rural roads.
4. Night driving.
5. Dual carriageways.
6. Motorways.

8.   M.O.T. Certificate.

     a. This lasts for one year and is needed to tax your car.
     b. Having no M.O.T. can invalidate insurance.
     c. Cars over 3 years old must have a valid M.O.T. certificate, (over 4 years old in Northern Ireland).
     d. No M.O.T. means you cannot renew your tax.

9.   Vehicle Service Book.

The Service History Book is a record of when a car is serviced at a garage.

10.   To tax your car you must have;

     a. A valid insurance certificate.
     b. Valid M.O.T. if over 3 years old.
     c. The car registration document (V5C).

11.   To supervise learner drivers you must be; a fully qualified driver aged 21 or over and must have passed your driving test for over 3 years.

12.   Vehicle Handbook.

The Vehicle Handbook gives information about the car. It explains about the car's tyre pressures, controls on the vehicle, specifications etc.

13.   The maximum fine for driving with no insurance is unlimited.

14.   You must produce your documents if asked by the Police within 7 days, e.g. the insurance and M.O.T. certificate, your driving licence and the Vehicle Registration Document (V5C).

15.   You must notify the D.V.L.A. when: -

     a. Your health affects your driving.
     b. You change your vehicle.
     c. Your eyesight deteriorates.

Deteriorating eyesight does not mean informing the D.V.L.A. of normal deterioration as long as you can read a number plate from 67 feet or 20 metres with or without glasses in good daylight. It means other conditions generally specified by an eye specialist or doctor.

d. You change address.

e. You have modifications done to the vehicle.

16. To drive on the road legally you must have a signed valid driving licence, your car taxed and have proper insurance cover e.g. the car must be insured for your use. (In October 2014 paper tax discs were abolished and information is now stored electronically).

Copy of a tax disc now abolished.

17. You are allowed to drive with no M.O.T. when driving to a pre-arranged appointment at an M.O.T. Centre.

It is illegal to drive a car over 3 years old with no M.O.T. (4 years in Northern Ireland). If a car needs to be repaired to pass the M.O.T and has no M.O.T then if the car is roadworthy but needs to be driven to a testing station, an appointment must be made prior to driving. If stopped by the police on the way to the appointment, the police can check with the testing station and you will have proof. If no M.O.T. appointment has been made then the driver is breaking the law.

18. The registered keeper is responsible for up-dating any changes on the Registration Document (V5C).

19. When a learner driver passes the driving test they are on two years' probation. This means if they get 6 penalty points or more, they must re-apply for a provisional driving licence and retake both theory and practical driving tests.

20. The registered keeper of the vehicle is responsible for paying the vehicle excise duty (road tax).

CASE STUDY

Ashleigh has just passed her test and buys a second hand car. The problem is it needs repairs and has no M.O.T. Her father is a mechanic so repairs her car and takes it to the garage for the M.O.T. The car passes the M.O.T. She needs to be insured so she asks the advice of her parents. She gets the insurance with an excess of £100 on her policy. The broker issues Ashleigh with a cover note.

Q.1. If the car has no M.O.T. and Ashleigh drives it – what can this affect?
Mark one answer.

a. The bodywork of the car.
b. Her driving licence.
c. Her registration document.
d. Her insurance.

Q.2. What is the minimum insurance that Ashleigh can buy?
Mark one answer.

a. Third party fire and theft.
b. Fully comprehensive.
c. Third party.
d. Personal accident.

Q.3. What is a cover note?
Mark one answer.

a. It is a temporary insurance document.
b. It is the policy document.
c. It is an M.O.T. document.
d. It is a road tax document.

Q.4. What is the £100 excess on her insurance?
Mark one answer.

a. She will have to pay the first £100 in the event of a claim.
b. She will get a discount of £100 off her policy if she does not claim.
c. She will get a £100 bonus after driving for one year accident free.
d. It pays for the arrangement of her insurance cover.

Chapter 13

INCIDENTS & ACCIDENTS

1. Rumble strips/devices warn of a hazard or danger and encourage drivers to reduce speed.

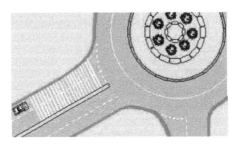

Rumble strips/devices are raised strips across the road surface. They can be found on the approach to roundabouts, outside schools, in built up areas etc. They are to make the driver aware of their speed and encourage them to reduce speed. They warn of hazards.

2. Before driving through a tunnel, switch on the radio.

Before driving through a tunnel, well before approaching the tunnel it could be wise to tune into a local radio station for traffic information. This could warn of any accidents, delays, diversions etc.

3. When attempting to resuscitate an injured person the chest compressions are 100 – 120 per minute – 5 to 6 centimeters or 2½ inches.

4. At the scene of an accident, if a casualty is unconscious, check their breathing for a minimum time of 10 seconds.

5. Signs of shock in a casualty can be sweating/pale grey skin, a rapid pulse and shallow breathing.

6. Variable message signs before tunnels and ATM's (Active Traffic Management area) warn of incidents, collisions or congestion ahead. Keep a lookout for changing signs.

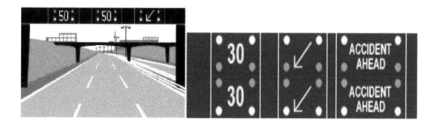

Active Traffic Management (ATM) Consists of traffic monitoring, CCTV camera's watch for accidents happening on motorways. Active traffic management deals with;
Accident control
Different/variable message signs.
Control of lane signals.
Variable/Different speed limit signs.
Information for drivers.
History of what has happened ahead e.g. incidents/accidents.

7. Burns should be cooled with clean water or a non-toxic liquid for a minimum of 10 minutes.

8. Damage to property or injury to another person must be reported to police within 24 hours.

9. In an incident do not move injured people if the area is safe. Keep them in the car. Only move them if there is further danger.

10. Always think A.B.C. `airway - breathing - circulation` when checking injured people. If a person is unconscious follow the DRABC code.

If an injured person is unconscious follow the DR ABC rules;

    D. = Danger - check for danger before approaching an accident.
    R. = Response - gently shake a shoulder to get a response.
    A. = Airway - check the airway is clear.
    B. = Check that the injured person is breathing.
    C. = Compressions – 5-6 cms at a rate of 100-120 per minute.

If you need to try to resuscitate a person, pinch their nostrils gently before performing the procedure.

11. Do not remove anything sticking to a burn.

12. If a casualty is bleeding badly from an arm or leg wound, raise the limb above the level of the heart and apply firm pressure to reduce the flow of blood.

13. If you breakdown on a level crossing, get passengers and yourself out of the car and get clear of the crossing. If the vehicle operator tells you to move the vehicle, then do so.

14. Never remove a motorcyclist's helmet if injured in a crash, it may cause more injury.

If a motorcyclist is injured and unconscious never remove their helmet as this could cause further injury. Only remove it if you deem it essential.

15. Always keep a safe distance from the vehicle in front.

Rule 126: Use a fixed point to help measure a two-second gap

A useful tip is to use a 2 second gap between your vehicle and the one in front in good conditions, increase to a 4 second gap (double) in wet conditions and up to 10 times if driving in icy weather.

16. Remove sunglasses before driving through a tunnel.

Before driving through a dark tunnel remove any sunglasses as the quick change from light to dark may not give your eyes time to adjust and may affect your visibility.

17. In an accident find the other drivers: -
    a. Name, address and telephone number.
    b. Details of their insurance.
    c. The make and registration number of their vehicle.
    d. Who owns the vehicle.

18. Place a warning triangle 45 metres (147 feet) behind the vehicle.

Warning triangles need to be placed a distance away (45 metres 147 feet) from the hazard so other drivers are alerted in good time to potential danger. The accident/incident could also be around a bend or in a hidden dip, so plenty of warning to make other motorists aware is important.

19. Use dipped headlights in tunnels.

20. Use hazard lights to warn of an incident ahead or when broken down and blocking the road.

21. Never try to pick up anything on a motorway.

When driving on a motorway, if you see something fall from another vehicle or from your own vehicle, or there is something unusual on the road, never stop to try and retrieve the item as motorways have fast moving traffic. Even if the motorway is empty, traffic could appear at any time. Go to an emergency telephone and report the situation.

22. Sometimes police need to check documents after an accident. They may need the M.O.T. certificate, insurance certificate and driving licence.

23. If there are problems when driving in a tunnel e.g. accidents or breakdowns – switch on your hazard warning lights.

24. If a tyre bursts, you should hold the steering wheel firmly and let the vehicle roll to a stop. If on a motorway, pull up onto the hard shoulder and seek assistance.

25. The hard shoulder on motorways is to be used only in emergencies and breakdowns or when directed.

Hard shoulders on motorways are only to be used in emergency situations such as vehicle breakdowns or if directed to do so by Police or Highways Agency Officers.

26. If there is an accident - keep people warm and comfortable, do not leave them alone and keep them calm. Reassure them constantly.

27. Non toxic liquid is not poisonous e.g. water.

28. After a collision - first stop, then warn other traffic.

29. After an incident if there is damage or injury and there is no-one around, report it to the police within 24 hours.

30. At the scene of an accident do not put yourself at risk.

31. On a motorway when using an emergency telephone, you will be asked for:-
    The number of the phone you are using.
    Details of yourself and your vehicle.
    If you are a member of a breakdown organisation e.g. AA, RAC, Green Flag etc.

32. A disabled person may display a help pennant.

*If a disabled person is driving and breaks down, they may not be able to vacate their vehicle and seek help. In this situation they may display a pennant with the word **HELP** on. This is may be attached to a car door with a wire.*

33. If your vehicle catches fire in a tunnel and can still be driven, try to drive it out and if possible put the fire out.

If this is not possible, get passengers clear and call the Fire Brigade. Remember to switch off the engine and switch on the hazard warning lights.

34. It is useful to carry a first aid kit, warning triangle and a fire extinguisher in your vehicle for emergencies.

35. If a casualty is a small child and is not breathing, you must check their airway then give chest compressions, either using one hand or 2 fingers for a baby. Breathe very gently into their mouth.

36. Do not move anyone who has injured their back - call the emergency services.

37. Be aware when following a vehicle displaying a dangerous chemicals sign.

38. Check your vehicle if you smell a strong smell of petrol.

39. If any warning light comes on the instrument panel – check it out.

CASE STUDY

While driving, Julie arrives at the scene of an accident, three cars and a motorbike are involved. She needs to warn other traffic as she is the first to witness the accident. There are casualties. One is unconscious and not breathing, another is bleeding heavily.

Q.1. Julie needs to decide what to do first. What is the first thing Julie should do?
Mark one answer.

a. Help the motorcyclist.
b. Leave as she can't help.
c. Warn other traffic.
d. Make people comfortable.

Q.2. Julie decides she needs to give compressions to the unconscious person. How deep should the compressions be?
Mark one answer.

a. 2-3 cms.
b. 3-4 cms.
c. 5-6 cms.
d. 9-10 cms.

Q.3. At what rate should she give the compressions?
Mark one answer.

a. 20 per minute.
b. 50 per minute.
c. 80 per minute.
d. 100-120 per minute.

Q.4. Which documents would the police ask to see from the people involved in the accident?
Mark one answer.

a. Driving licence and M.O.T. certificate.
b. Insurance certificate and birth certificate.
c. Insurance certificate and driving licence.
d. Vehicle Registration document and M.O.T. certificate.

Chapter 14

UNDERSTANDING VEHICLE LOADING

1. If a caravan or trailer swerves or snakes, ease off the gas/accelerator to reduce speed gently.

2. Heavy loads on a roof rack may reduce stability and affect steering and control. All loads should be securely fastened before driving.

3. On a three lane motorway or dual carriageway when towing, use only the left and centre lanes and do not drive above 60mph.

4. A breakaway cable can be an extra safety device fitted to the braking system.

It is a legal requirement that braked trailers must be fitted with a breakaway cable. This must be attached to the towing vehicle so that if the trailer becomes detached, the breakaway cable will operate the trailers brakes.

5. Inflate the tyres to more than the normal pressure when driving long distances or carrying heavy loads.

6. A stabiliser fitted to the towbar can help vehicle handling and helps prevent snaking and can also help in crosswinds.

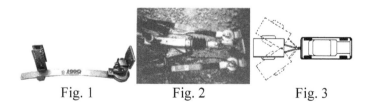

Fig. 1   Fig. 2   Fig. 3

Fig.4

The main purpose of a stabiliser (Fig.1 and Fig.2) is to stop a trailer or caravan from becoming unstable and 'snaking' from side to side (Fig.3). Snaking is when the axles of a caravan or trailer move out of line from the towing vehicle. When this happens the trailer/caravan tries to move back in line and it goes too far. This action starts the snaking from side to side. Unless the snaking is stopped, it will increase and cause the driver to lose control. Stabilisers must be checked at the start of each journey. Fig. 4 is a road sign showing possible crosswinds/side winds. These winds could affect a trailer or caravan's handling on the road.

7.   Passengers are not allowed to ride in a caravan being towed.

8.   Maximum nose weight of the vehicle tow ball can be found in the vehicle handbook.

Fig.5

Towballs are part of the couplings (Fig. 5) which are used to tow a trailer or caravan, the weight specified in the vehicle handbook must be adhered to for safety reasons. You must not tow more than your licence permits and you must not overload your vehicle or trailer.

9.   A load on the roof rack should be securely fastened when driving and not protruding.

10. The driver of the vehicle is responsible to make sure the vehicle is not overloaded.

11. Children under 3 years old should use a child seat with restraints. If no child seat is available, use an adult seat belt.

12. If transporting a dog in a vehicle, make sure it is suitably restrained by a harness or a dog cage.

Dogs should be suitably restrained when being transported in your vehicle by the use of a harness or a dog cage. These measures may help prevent you being injured by the animal if you are attempting a manoeuvre or have to stop quickly and also may prevent the animal distracting you whilst you are driving.

13. Carrying a load or pulling a trailer may require you to adjust the headlights on your vehicle.

Additional information

The following are useful additions to help with vehicle loading. Corner steadies (Fig. 1) are used to steady a caravan or trailer when parked. The jockey wheel (Fig. 2) makes it easier to hook the tow vehicle onto the trailer. ABS (Anti-lock brakes) reduces the risk of skidding and power steering is used to supplement the drivers' effort in turning the steering wheel.

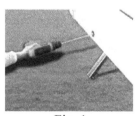

Fig. 1   Fig. 2

CASE STUDY

Alan is taking his family on a caravan holiday. The drive will include motorways and country roads. He hooks up the caravan and loads extras onto the roof rack. He checks everything to make sure all is safe following advice from different sources.

Q.1. Can Alan allow one or more of his passengers to ride in the caravan when being towed?
Mark one answer.

a. Yes, all of them permitted.
b. Yes, but only one person is permitted.
c. None are allowed at any time when being towed.
d. Only if the towing vehicle is full.

Q.2. What extra safety device could Alan use when towing the caravan?
Mark one answer.

a. Corner steadies.
b. A breakaway cable.
c. A jockey wheel.
d. Winter tyres.

Q.3. Alan has to drive on a 3 lane section of motorway. Which lanes can he use?
Mark one answer.

a. The hard shoulder and left lane.
b. All 3 lanes.
c. The left and centre lane.
d. The hard shoulder and right lane.

Q.4. When Alan couples the caravan up to the towing vehicle he needs to know the maximum nose weight of the tow ball. Where can he find this?
Mark one answer.

a. On the M.O.T. certificate.
b. In the service book.
c. On the Registration document.
d. In the vehicle handbook.

CASE STUDY ANSWERS

BEING ALERT
Q.1. b. Because it can distract from his driving if he adjusts it on route.
Q.2. c. He needs to make sure the driver of the lorry can see him in his mirror.
Q.3. d. Stop at a service area, rest and have a caffeinated drink.
Q.4. c. Bar markings would be on the approach.

GOOD DRIVING ATTITUDES
Q.1. a. 4 seconds.
Q.2. b. To make sure she can be seen by other traffic.
Q.3. c. Pelican.
Q.4. b. Green.

VEHICLE SAFETY
Q.1. c. 1.6mm.
Q.2. a. Braking and steering.
Q.3. b. Press down on the front corner of the car, to see if it continues to bounce.
Q.4. c. To protect the baby from harm, if the car is involved in an accident.

UNDERSTANDING SAFETY MARGINS
Q.1. b. Side winds are more dangerous on open stretches of road.
Q.2. a. Strong winds can affect motorcyclists, cyclists and high sided vehicles more than cars.
Q.3. b. Bright sunlight can dazzle and other drivers may not see his indicators.
Q.4. b. To avoid brake fade.

BEING AWARE OF HAZARDS
Q.1. b. Traffic calming measures.
Q.2. c. The cyclist may wobble or swerve.
Q.3. b. Because she knows she would be breaking the law and restricting visibility if she parks on them.
Q.4. b. 8mph.

OTHER VULNERABLE ROAD USERS
Q.1. b. It improves your driving skills and reduces risks of collisions.
Q.2. a. They provide a warning to drivers to slow down approaching the roundabout.

Q.3. b. Paul knows the cyclist may take a different course on the roundabout because he is more vulnerable.

Q.4. c. Ignore the drivers error and stay calm.

DIFFERENT TYPES OF VEHICLE
Q.1. b. Extended-arm side mirror.
Q.2. b. Cars.
Q.3. c. 100 metres.
Q.4. d. Dipped headlights.

VEHICLE HANDLING IN ROAD CONDITIONS
Q.1. b. Passing Places.
Q.2. c. His visibility is reduced because of the fading light.
Q.3. d. Pedestrians.
Q.4. a. To use the engine as a brake.

KNOWING THE RULES OF MOTORWAYS
Q.1. c. The left lane.
Q.2. b. 60 mph.
Q.3. d. Only the middle and left lane.
Q.4. d. Breakdowns and emergencies.

KNOWING THE RULES OF THE ROAD
Q.1. c. Amber.
Q.2. c. Either on the right or left.
Q.3. c. It is for vehicles which have two or more occupants.
Q.4. b. 10 Metres (15 Metres in Northern Ireland).

KNOWING YOUR ROAD & TRAFFIC SIGNS
Q.1. a. No motor vehicles.
Q.2. d. Do not cross the lines.
Q.3. a. 60mph.
Q.4. c. Tourist information.

RELEVANT DRIVING DOCUMENTS
Q.1 d. The insurance.
Q.2 c. Third party.
Q.3 a. It is a temporary insurance document.
Q.4 a. She will have to pay the first £100 in the event of a claim.

INCIDENTS & ACCIDENTS

Q.1. c. Warn other traffic.

Q.2. c. 5-6 cms.

Q.3. d. 100-120 per minute.

Q.4. d. Vehicle Registration document and M.O.T. certificate.

UNDERSTANDING VEHICLE LOADING

Q.1. c. None are allowed at any time when being towed.

Q.2. b. A breakaway cable.

Q.3. c. The left and centre lane.

Q.4. d. In the vehicle handbook.